Design for Change

The Architecture of DEGW

Design for Change
The Architecture of DEGW

with contributions by

Francis Duffy
Stephen Greenberg
Jeremy Myerson
Kenneth Powell
Tony Thomson
and
John Worthington

Watermark Publications
Haslemere

Birkhäuser Verlag
Basel · Boston · Berlin

Designed and co-ordinated by Ian Lambot.
Translated from English into German by Caroline
Gutbrod.

A CIP catalogue record for this book is available from
the Library of Congress, Washington DC, USA.

Deutsche Bibliothek Cataloguing-in-Publication Data
Design for change: the architecture of DEGW / with
contributions by Francis Duffy ... -Basel ; Boston ;
Berlin : Birkhäuser ; Haslemere : Watermark, 1998
    Dt. Ausg. u.d.T.: Flexible Gebäude
    ISBN 3-7643-5738-X (Basel)
    ISBN 0-8176-5738-X (Boston)

© 1998 Birkhäuser – Verlag für Architektur,
PO Box 133, CH-4010 Basel, Switzerland and
Watermark Publications (UK) Limited,
PO Box 92, Haslemere, Surrey GU27 2YQ

Printed on acid-free paper produced from chlorine free
pulp. TCF ∞
Printed in Italy.

ISBN 3-7643-5738-X

9 8 7 6 5 4 3 2 1

Contents

Foreword

I would like to dedicate this book to all the talented people who have worked for DEGW over the last quarter of a century, both in the practice's various manifestations – JFN UK, Duffy Lange Giffone Worthington, Duffy Eley Giffone Worthington, the DEGW Partnership or DEGW plc – and in its many diverse locations – including Amersfoort, Athens, Berlin, Brussels, Glasgow, London, Madrid, Mexico City, Milan, New York, Paris and Sydney. A million thanks to you all.

Special thanks are due to Francis Duffy, Stephen Greenberg, Tony Thomson and John Worthington, all members of the practice who have helped by taking responsibility for writing major parts of *Design for Change*. Kenneth Powell wrote the case studies describing DEGW's projects, while Mick Bedford, Stephen Bradley, Colin Cave, Andrew Harrison, David Jenkin, Despina Katsikakis, Kate Lee, Graham Parsey, Philip Tidd and Graham Vickers helped in planning the book, in developing the text and in selecting the projects and illustrations. Many thanks to them, and also to Jeremy Myerson for giving the book a sound structure in its early stages and for writing the introduction.

The book would probably not have appeared, and certainly would not have been so handsome, without the meticulous design, painstaking picture research and thoughtful editing undertaken by Ian Lambot.

DEGW is now part of the Twijnstra Gudde group of companies. This union benefits DEGW by giving the practice access to a broader range of consultancy and management skills. Meanwhile, Twijnstra Gudde and DEGW are developing new ways of serving clients through our expanding international network. This book is a record of some of these new ideas.

DEGW has always been well known for stimulating change. The process continues with Twijnstra Gudde. I regard this book not so much as a record of something completed, but rather as the first chapter of an ever unfolding story.

Jan Regterschot
Director Twijnstra Gudde

The Goethe Galerie, at the heart of the revived Carl Zeiss works in Jena: just one in a series of recent high-profile projects that have established DEGW's credentials as design architects, as well as space-planners and masterplanners.

The great glazed roof of the Goethe Galerie was designed in association with engineer-architect IFB Dr Braschel GmbH.

Introduction

Architects of buildings and designers of interiors are living in troubling times. The skills, outlooks and methodologies which armed and sustained them for much of this century seem far less secure given the complex, unpredictable and downright scary economic and technological scenarios envisaged for the first years of the twenty-first century.

Old certainties are being eroded and new knowledge demanded as architects struggle to cope with the constant realignments imposed by clients and contractors in the building process, and by users everywhere, in places and spaces for living and working. From this point of view, the idea of signature architecture as lasting for ever – monolithic and immune to the forces of change – has been exposed as impractical and irrelevant.

Working in the library at DEGW: the pursuit of new architectural knowledge is a central concern within the practice.

Designers, working in a more responsive and less structured environment, face different versions of the same challenges.

But it is the profession of architecture that has been so painfully slow to change. It is turning slowly, like a giant oil tanker on the ocean, its arc is so wide as to be almost imperceptible. Generating the new knowledge, the new ideas and new approaches that are required simply to

DEGW's London headquarters at Porters North: the firm has had a significant influence on the course of contemporary architecture.

stay in touch in the construction industry – never mind on top – takes enormous energy and is an objective far easier to describe than to achieve.

In this context, the architectural practice of DEGW can be seen as a tugboat – busy, highly mobile and exercising a quite disproportionate influence to its size – ceaseless in its efforts to guide the mother ship of architecture in a new direction. Steering a course that has constantly nagged the conscience of other architects around the world, DEGW has forced other design practices to re-evaluate their work in the light of its own design initiatives and research discoveries.

Most leading architectural practices about whom monographs are written are renowned for the powerful images or objects they create in the land- or cityscape, and in the mind's eye of that holy trinity of patrons, planners and pundits. But DEGW is different. It has constantly reminded us that it is not enough simply to design innovative architectural form; it is what goes on inside buildings over time that creates the real drama, not just the shell. It is not enough, either, just to design beautiful buildings which are perfect at the freeze-frame point of completion. Their performance over time and in response to the changing needs of users must be monitored and measured.

Not that DEGW is in any way uninterested in the aesthetic impact of buildings, as the case studies in this book demonstrate. In a time of intense architectural activity, DEGW is as alert to the resonance of architectural imagery as any of its peers. But DEGW's special contribution has been to exploit and then to transcend conventional architectural skills to generate new knowledge about how organisations and individuals use buildings, to classify generic building types so that comparisons can be made, and to develop tools to measure and evaluate the response of buildings to the needs of their users over time.

DEGW is, therefore, as much concerned with an 'architecture of ideas' as with formal imagery. It is the interweaving of ideas with architecture that establishes the governing theme of this book: design for change. Change has become the greatest challenge, aesthetic as well as programmatic, of contemporary architecture.

The Victorian philanthropists might have had unbending ideas about the unchanging nature of their social and educational institutions. The giant pre-war industrial giants – Hoover, Chrysler and so on – might have thought their corporate factory-palaces would last for ever. But, today, there is hardly an organisation on earth that would dare believe that it is immune from radical and punishing change. To conceive, design and construct buildings and interiors capable of adapting to and absorbing accelerating change is the ultimate test for the architect and one for which the architectural precedents of an increasingly style-obsessed century offer little encouragement.

Since the practice was first established in London in 1971 – for the first three years under the name JFN as an offshoot of one of the leading New York space planners of the period – DEGW has always been much more interested in the social phenomena of change than the chimera of a fixed and definitive style. Reasons for this can be found in the firm's collective history which is at least as close to the impatient, fast-moving, future-seeking rhythm of New York as to the calmer, more retrospective European design tradition. This is very unusual for a European practice and explains why DEGW today is established in London, New York and Sydney as well as in Glasgow, Paris, Berlin, Madrid, Milan, Brussels and Amersfoort.

The original, architect-trained partners of DEGW – Francis Duffy, Luigi Giffone and John Worthington – all owe their approach to this

11

Glazing detail from DEGW's refurbishment of the DTI offices in London: pushing boundaries in practice as well as theory.

critical mixture of North American and European experiences. Giffone's architectural and engineering education and subsequent practice in Rome, for example, made him a sensitive generalist designer of the Italian tradition who feels equally comfortable designing sunglasses or cities. This breadth of vision was considerably enhanced by a decade in North America with time spent in studios as diverse as Taliesen West and Corporate Image Consultants in New York.

Worthington, Duffy and Peter Eley – who joined the practice in 1974 – studied together at the Architectural Association in London and subsequently in sequence as Harkness Fellows in the United States. Their joint backgrounds are instructive. Early '60s architectural education in Britain paid scant attention to the past. The Modern Movement aimed to brush away the cobwebs of history, rethink from first principles and provide 'heroic' statements. Duffy, in particular, recalls belonging as a student at the AA, to a "tiny, fiercely independent, self-governing world" in which "fragments of a wider world of knowledge – cultural history, sociology, design methodology – were ruthlessly and single-mindedly picked up and put to use solely in the cause of architecture. How buildings looked, how they were drawn and how they could be built in ever more innovative ways were practically all that we cared about".

This was increasingly an architectural period of grand, centrally-planned master strategies that aimed to deliver democratic solutions to meet the needs of the welfare state using the methods of industrial mass production – although influences as diverse as Cedric Price, Robert Maxwell, Roy Landau and Alan Colquhoun were welcome counter-forces. However, John Worthington's time

DEGW's refurbishment of the Victoria Street offices of the Department of Trade and Industry, in London, reflects a focus on the practical issues of construction as well as an 'architecture of ideas'. In addition to a total overhaul of the office floors, the project entailed the creation of a new entrance pavilion.

generic plans
two and three storey houses

Generic Plans,
an early expres-
sion of Francis
Duffy's lifelong
interest in space
planning which
he co-authored
for the National
Housing Associ-
ation in the mid-
1960s.

at the Universities of Pennsylvania and Berkeley provided a critical exposure to urban design and systems thinking through the work of Crane, Rapkin, Davidoff, Achoff, Alexander, Rittel and, above all, Louis Kahn.

This was followed through by Peter Eley, who undertook the two-year urban design course at Philadelphia, and by Francis Duffy, who also went to Berkeley. Duffy absorbed the lessons of Rittel and Alexander, and subsequently completed his doctorate at Princeton during the heyday of Graves, Gwathmey, Eisenman, Frampton, Vidler – though, academically at least, he worked

A selection of
DEGW's recent
workplace de-
signs: while
other architects
have neglected
the dynamics of
the office interi-
or, DEGW has
specialised in
them.

under the more sociologically inclined influence of Geddes and Gutman.

North America provided the perspective, the breadth of cultural experience and the intellectual rigour that enabled DEGW's founding partners to think critically about the wider role of architects from the very beginning of the practice. Significantly, from the start, DEGW has continued to attract American born and educated designers – Luigi Mangano, who left Italy to work for SOM in Washington DC; Despina Katsikakis, brought up in Chicago and educated as an architect there

and at the AA; Andrew Laing, who got his doctorate at MIT; Stephen Greenberg, an alumnus of the Harvard Graduate School of Design; Holli Rowan and many others.

Francis Duffy says of his time in New York, working at JFN alongside the best office designers and space planners of the late 1960s: "I went to mock and stayed to pray". Nothing in his conventional architectural education had prepared him for this exposure to the corporate world, with its pressures of time and money, with its emphasis on high design standards as well as on excellent programming or brief writing. "Above everything else, I learned that client organisations are in a constant state of change. The New York space planners, were, I believe, the first designers to really appreciate this. And that was 30 years ago."

From the time of his award-winning diploma thesis at the AA, Duffy had shown not only a clear talent as a designer but also an acute understanding that innovation stemmed as much from a reappraisal of the brief and an understanding of users, as from the ordering of space. His Princeton doctoral thesis was a masterly merging of an understanding of both space and organisational design characteristics as they interacted through time.

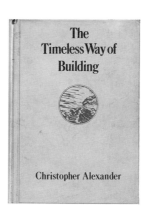

Christopher Alexander's views on buildings, time and 'pattern language' have proved influential throughout DEGW's 30 years of practice.

The outcome, which focused on the typology of the commercial North American office – epitomised by the Seagram Building – layered briefing and design decisions according to their life cycle and their sequence in the building's design and production process. Duffy defined the original sequence as follows: shell, services, scenery, settings. Crucially, he distinguished between different levels of longevity in office design – from the five-year duration of the scenery of the office interior through 15 years for services to the 50-year life of a building shell. Investment, he noted, would increasingly switch from shell to scenery. And so it proved.

Thirty years on, Duffy's thesis is still the only one I know of that is uncomplicated enough to be explained in two minutes on the back of an envelope, yet remains enormously relevant to today's buildings and organisations. It was a powerful, simple and elegant theory that related the classic sociological dimensions of interaction and bureaucracy to the physical properties of an office – its degree of enclosure, the quality of its finishes and so on – and showed how these were used to accentuate differences in status. The same kind

of model can be applied as well to the design of cities as to furniture. Analytical thinking, related directly to design, has informed the direction of DEGW over three decades in its quest to be an outstanding consultancy as well as an excellent design practice.

I first came into contact with the practice in its Marylebone headquarters in the early 1980s when DEGW was barely a decade old. It was a crowded seminar on a hot London night. The subject was the dynamics of the office environment – not a topic which other architects generally got excited about – and the atmosphere was electric. It has often been said that DEGW resembles a university in its focus on academic research and publishing; here was evidence of radical campus politics aimed at forcing workplace architects and designers to ask searching questions of themselves. People tore into each other with real vigour that night. Office interiors, the practice's prime focus, really mattered.

DEGW's formative years in the 1970s coincided with a rise of consumer and workers' rights in Britain, and at least some of that flavour influenced its strong commitment to user consultation and participation in both offices and neighbourhood regeneration schemes. Certainly the social democracy embodied in such early DEGW schemes as Unipart – a lively, colourful warehouse fit-out for a company anxious to escape the institutionalised industrial relations conflict of the UK motor industry – could not have happened but for the mood of the time.

But as DEGW established the disciplines of space planning and programming (brief writing) in Europe during the 1970s and early '80s, it also drew heavily on the technologies and language of American planning and business studies. Key concepts – such as time budgeting (Chapin), activity mapping (Ronnels), advocacy planning

DEGW's design for a new swimming pool at Bradfield College, 1995. As different types of workplace become 'learning environments' of one sort or another, so DEGW's once-singular focus on the office is rapidly widening to embrace a broad range of educational and leisure interiors which transcend conventional building types.

Boardroom of the Prudential headquarters in London, 1993, where DEGW integrated high-tech services into a listed interior.

(Davidoff), participative design (Sanoff), studies of building use (Cooper) and, above all, the application of scientific methodology to architectural study (Rittel) – were transferred and adapted most obviously to the task of assessing and redesigning the changing environment of office work.

The outcome was an identifiable DEGW approach to office design founded on matching building and organisational characteristics, post-occupancy evaluation, space budgeting and participatory briefing. These techniques – which first surfaced in the DEGW book *Planning Office Space* (Architectural Press, 1976) – were honed in the workshop of the corporate office world and were to become equally valuable in the practice's later work in urban planning and new building design. Today, they are being applied with increasing frequency in other sectors, such as universities, laboratories, museums, exhibition design and even housing and health. What began as a singular focus on the office is inevitably widening as increasingly ubiquitous information technology is rapidly turning *all* environments into learning environments. The logic of DEGW's development must transcend conventional building types.

Significantly, in learning to enjoy dealing directly with the personal micro-politics of the office interior, in which every participant has traditionally owned or desired to own individual space, DEGW has been inspired to develop a transparent, democratic, bottom-up approach to planning both buildings and cities – using whatever methodologies for user consultation and evaluation come to hand. This is in stark contrast to the opaque, top-down, centralist, take-it-or-leave-it approach so common in conventional building procurement and city planning. The urge to publish and share knowledge about architectural theory and practice, evident from early on,

would also become a defining characteristic of DEGW. Indeed, its record of publication continues to be outstanding, not least because of the discovery that journalism can be a most effective way of developing ideas in the context of action.

Against this background, how, then, can one do justice to such an unusual and important design practice in a new book on its latest work? To filter DEGW's new building and interior designs through the eye of one external critic would have been inappropriate – and philosophically wrong – for a design practice of such diversity. Far better to create a book out of the conversations, the writings, the plans, the diagrams and the drawings of the different specialists – the architects, interior designers, ergonomists, psychologists, engineers, consultants, anthropologists, social researchers, computer and furniture specialists – who make DEGW what it is today.

Consequently, *Design For Change: The Architecture of DEGW* consists of two kinds of contribution: first, a series of essays, written by different DEGW people, that is intended to capture some of the main theoretical ideas that characterise the thinking of the practice; and second, a parallel series of narratives, written by Kenneth Powell, about different aspects of the design and architectural work of the practice, that present in a series of interconnected case studies the practical and physical consequences of these 'big' ideas. Time in architecture is the first and, perhaps, the most important essay topic. While other architects have ignored the transience of their work, time has definitively shaped DEGW's outlook, because of the practice's extensive experience of accommodating organisational change.

The second essay deals with the difficulties and opportunities of identifying the needs of the user, so often forgotten in architectural education but never by DEGW. The third essay turns

DEGW has successfully adapted the democratic, bottom-up approach to dealing with the micropolitics of the office to the much larger macro-scale of city planning. User behaviour and participation is a key issue, as in this masterplan for the Rummelsburgerbucht area of former East Berlin.

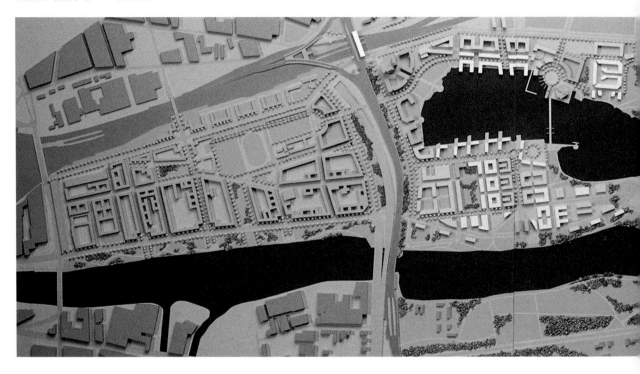

our attention to DEGW's comparative typological approach to building design and explains the practical as well as the theoretical benefits of generic types in architecture and interior design. Essay four presents the evolution of DEGW's architecture in terms of the story of light and air. It discusses ways in which organisational flexibility can be maintained amid the delicately balanced integration of architectural form and environmental services. Finally, the fifth essay deals with the idea of the regeneration of cities. In particular, it looks at the impact of new technology on redundant buildings, typically in decayed city centres, and shows how a careful blend of thoughtful conservation and sympathetic redevelopment can bring forth new life.

The more or less abstract concepts dealt with in the essays – time, the user, typologies, light

and air, and regeneration – all share a direct connection to the practical strategies which enable DEGW's architects to design for change. These strategies are discussed in the main essays and elaborated in the case studies. More than a dozen of the practice's major players have contributed, either by writing or by interview, directly to this book. Many more members of DEGW, past and present, have contributed in another and equally important way – through their ideas and their designs. If, as a result, this book seems different, it is because DEGW really has been devised as a different kind of collaborative architectural practice. The processes by which both DEGW and this record of the practice's work have been invented and produced – whatever else one might say about the results – are certainly not normal in architecture.

It is important to understand, at the outset, DEGW's dual role as consultants and designers.

An early sketch for the Camelia Botnar laboratories: the relationship between user requirements, services and design was a key concern from the outset.

The bimodal nature of the practice is intended to ensure that design proposals are always being tested by research and that consultancy is constantly being challenged by built reality. The criticality for DEGW of this two-way connection has created an environment in which research into the relation between user requirements and design has always flourished. Some of this research has been carried out for single clients, but another powerful way of conducting research in the context of action has been multi-client studies in which a group of clients share costs and participate directly in the direction of the research.

The first such study carried out by DEGW was ORBIT (Office Research, Buildings and Information Technology) in 1981/82, which looked at the impact of information technology (IT) on organisational structure and building design. ORBIT, and the subsequent North American version ORBIT 2, were highly influential in establishing new parameters for office buildings to enable them to cope both with IT and with the changing nature of corporate structures in the UK and the USA.

While the ORBIT studies were under way, DEGW pioneered in London systematic ways of appraising the design and spatial performance of office buildings. Initially, these were used by developer clients to assess how well their new city-centre or business park office buildings met the emerging profiles of demand in the respective client sectors, but increasingly they have become a service to other architects and to user clients. Published studies such as *Eleven Contemporary Office Buildings* (1985), *Meeting the Needs of Modern Industry* (1985), *Trading in Three Cities* (1988) and *The Changing City* (1989) resulted from this research focus.

In 1991, another multi-client study, *The Responsible Workplace*, carried out in collaboration with the Building Research Establishment, highlighted yet further consequences of the information technology revolution on office design – the increasing fluidity in the use of time and space on organisational structures, on environmental design and on the management of office space. At the same time *The Intelligent Building in Europe* study (completed with Teknibank of Milan in 1992) investigated appropriate concepts for building intelligence in the European context, and undertook widespread market research with suppliers and end-users, establishing a new user-based definition of building intelligence.

The *Intelligent Buildings in South East Asia* study (1995/96), carried out with Ove Arup & Partners and Northcroft, further developed the

A landmark study, *ORBIT 2* explored the impact of information technology on organisational structure and building design in the USA and Canada.

EXECUTIVE OVERVIEW
An Overview of the Main Report and Supporting Volumes of the ORBIT-2 Project and Rating Process on Organisations, Buildings and Information Technology.

ORBIT2

Gerald Davis, Franklin Becker, Francis Duffy, William Sims

DEGW's hierarchical pyramid of building technologies in its study *The Intelligent Building in Europe* (1992) correctly anticipated that by the mid-1990s the computer-integrated building would take building intelligence to new heights.

Computer Integrated Building			Computer Intrgrated Building				1995
Integrated Systems		Building Automation Systems	Integrated communication Systems				1990
Multifunctional Systems	Security Access	HVAC etc	Text & Data	Voice	Image		1985
Single-function Dedicated Systems		Heating Ventilation Air	Electricity Water Lifts etc	EDP & Data	Telefax & Text	Voice	TV & Image	1980
	Security	Access					

Single apparatus

European model of building intelligence, determined its suitability for an Asian context and also examined global organisational and IT trends which will affect the next generation of intelligent buildings in the region. This is currently being followed up by *Intelligent Buildings in Latin America* (also with Northcroft and Arups) which is extending the concept of building intelligence to the scale of the city.

The year 1996 saw the completion of yet another major, multi-client research study, *New Environments for Working*, again in collaboration with the Building Research Establishment. This report established the requirements for new kinds of environmental servicing systems in offices capable of responding to the demands of organisations that are using both space and time in innovative ways.

These multi-client studies have been milestones in DEGW's intellectual development in learning how to design for change. Similar studies will undoubtedly continue to play an important role in the practice's global development. However, important as the practice's research tradition has been, its ultimate justification is only as the catalyst for continuously developing fresh and innovative designs to meet the emerging needs of real clients. The architectural and interior design work illustrated in the following pages has to be judged in its own right by the highest standards of international architecture, as well as in relation to client expectations. But the real test of the validity of this body of work from DEGW's own, far more stringent point of

The Changing Workplace surveyed more than 25 years of office design and thinking by Francis Duffy, revisiting his boldest predictions.

view is the degree to which each design initiative, each building, each interior, each exhibition, each product design, has been informed by the firm's research tradition. The question for DEGW is always whether the physical work of the practice has succeeded in testing, developing and making ideas real.

This habit of relating ideas to practice – and practice to ideas – has also helped DEGW to contribute to the broader field of architectural knowledge beyond the necessarily limiting concerns of running a busy practice. Francis Duffy, for example, was able to lead a wide-ranging strategic study of the future of the architectural profession in his role as President of the Royal Institute of British Architects; his final report in 1995 contained many recommendations on ways in which architecture could change from a "learned profession to a learning one" and become more relevant. John Worthington's roles as Professor of Architecture and Director of the Institute of Advanced Architectural Studies at the University of York (1992-97) and currently visiting professor

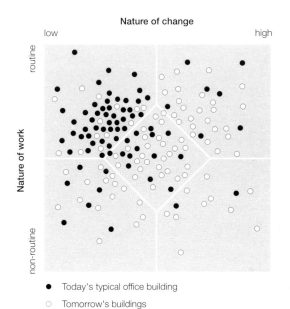

Nature of change

● Today's typical office building

○ Tomorrow's buildings

Diagrams from *New Environments for Working* show the nature of change as it affects both the shifting patterns of demand for office buildings *(left)* and a variety of different organisations *(below)*.

at the University of Sheffield have similarly been focused on developing strategies to ensure that architectural education and practice are capable of responding to the real needs of the age through better and more sophisticated briefing.

It is said that you can tell the mark of a good architectural firm by the company its keeps. DEGW has worked with some of the world's outstanding companies, from major institutions such as IBM and Olivetti to leading developers such as Stanhope, from furniture and product manufacturers such as Steelcase to famous architectural firms such as those run by Richard Rogers, Mario Bellini, Norman Foster, Daniel Libeskind, Renzo Piano or Terry Farrell. The reasons why these organisations have sought out DEGW's expertise are telling.

In her book *World Class: Thriving Locally in the Global Economy* (Simon & Schuster, New York 1995), Harvard professor Rosabeth Moss

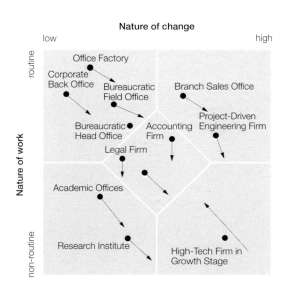

Entrance to the new Camelia Botnar laboratories at Great Ormond Street Hospital: realising ideas in built form is a key part of the DEGW mission.

Kanter describes what it takes to succeed in the customer-driven world economy. She talks of world-class companies being "rich in the three golden intangible assets, the three Cs of concepts, competence and connections. Those assets are hard to measure, but they are more critical for building the future than the tangible assets of capital, plant and equipment".

One can immediately see DEGW and its closest clients as exemplars of this thesis. As this book seeks to demonstrate, DEGW is a practice rich in concepts, chief among them being its emphasis on time-based design and its belief that it is folly for companies to invest in plant and equipment that are inflexible to change. However, DEGW is also focused on practice competence – realising its ideas in built form is an essential part of its mission. Finally, DEGW is renowned for the connections it has made between users, furniture, technology, buildings and cities, and for the techniques it has developed to effectively manage this interaction. In the process, DEGW, not once but several times, has been responsible

The evolution of DEGW's planned studies reveals that the ambition to investigate design for change remains undiminished.

for creating a totally new type of architecture for the working environment.

That DEGW, in 1997, after a long period of acquaintance and friendly co-operation, became part of the Dutch management consultancy Twijnstra Gudde (TG) is not just a manifestation of the practice's maturity and desire for growth. The merger is a means of continuing DEGW's unique design programme in a much more powerful way. It gives DEGW access to TG's formidable intellectual and client handling skills – 'upstream' in the architectural decision-making process, especially in information technology and human resources – which enable the practice to enrich its offerings in consultancy. And it also gives access to TG's equally impressive 'downstream' managerial capacity, particularly in programme and project management, thus hugely increasing DEGW's ability to deliver to its clients the right kind of architecture reliably, on time and at cost.

At the same time the new relationship allows DEGW to take advantage of TG's expertise in fields parallel to office design, such as health and

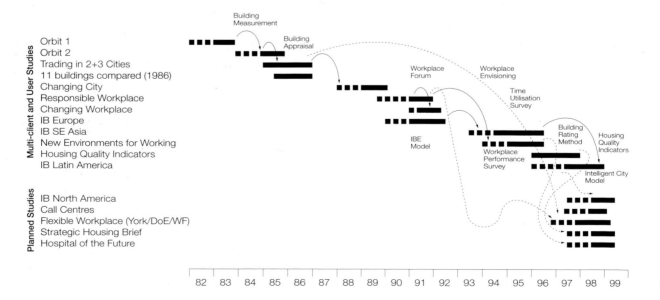

education. TG, of course, now has the reciprocal advantage of being able to use DEGW's European offices as well as the expanding network in North America and the Pacific. However, what cements this new relationship is not just a shared commercial and operational advantage. Both Twijnstra Gudde and DEGW share an intellectual approach to practice which allows individuals to develop within a collective 'college of knowledge', extending everyone's ability to learn within a supportive professional environment.

A concern to make connections and collaborate with others brings us back to the tugboat analogy made earlier in this introduction. DEGW's special relationship to the mother ship of the arts has been as a critic, a mentor and a guide. DEGW has proved to be a very special sort of tugboat with the power to nudge, to cajole and, hopefully, to set the architectural profession off safely in a new direction. However, the work presented in this book demonstrates two other things: first, that DEGW has also had the time and the energy and the talent to produce what is, by any standards, a formidable body of design; and second, that this unusual, tug-like architectural practice is equipped, not just with big engines for its size, but with a very powerful radar that can anticipate things happening at a distance and help to work out their consequences for both design and for clients.

DEGW's habit of systematic enquiry and willingness to share knowledge has given public and corporate clients, developers, end-users, and other architects and professionals, in Europe and around the world, the means to avoid obstacles and, by responding intelligently to change, to find a new way forward.

The Goethe Galerie, the centrepiece of DEGW's imaginative urban regeneration for the former East German city of Jena.

The scheme revels in the connections made between users, buildings, open spaces, technology and the city.

Organisational Change

Francis Duffy is an apostle of change – but change with a human face. It was General Ulysses S. Grant who said that the secret of success in war is being "the first-est with the mostest", but, Duffy believes, the saying is even more apposite in the modern business world, with its atmosphere of rapid change and relentless competition. As an architectural practice, DEGW is committed to design excellence and to the process of building, yet the extraordinary range of its interests highlights the tension between buildings – made to last – and the transient activities that go on inside them. This dynamic relationship has been the focus of DEGW's activities over the past quarter of a century.

As in the era of the Industrial Revolution, change is driven by technology and it is the revolution launched by new information technology which is currently transforming the place of work. The effects of this revolution were startlingly previewed in the early 1980s in DEGW's ORBIT studies, which underlined the absolute imperative for offices of the future to incorporate provision for rapid change. The pressure is now on every organisation to occupy flexible, high value space that promotes a sense of motivation and co-operative interaction among staff. Sometimes those objectives seem to be contradictory, but DEGW's mission is to prove that they are not.

Francis Duffy's early researches on the relation between organisational structure and office design led to work for the British civil service in the early 1970s. At that

The interior of BT's Stockley Park offices, as reconfigured by DEGW, provides a dynamic context for interaction and 'touch-down' working, with the café a natural focus.

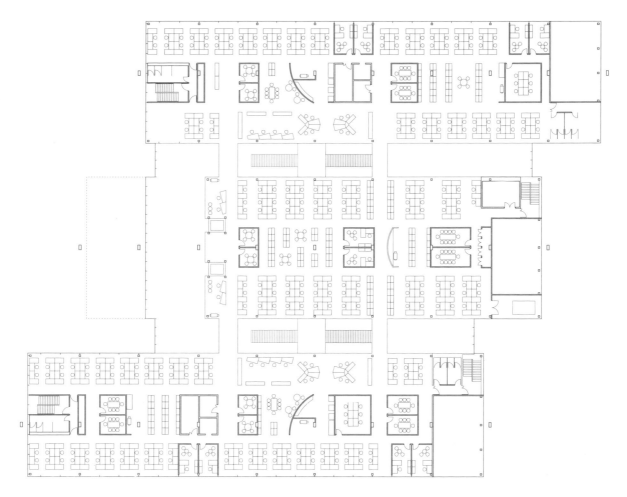

Designed by Foster and Partners, 5 The Longwalk at Stockley Park was designed to be used by one company or split into three separate units. BP subdivided much of the building into cellular offices, rather at odds with the architecture. BT and DEGW have reinstated an open layout.

time, space in offices was allocated not on the basis of convenience or need but on that of hierarchy: the size of an office, like the size of its desk, reflected the grading of individuals. "It was all very cosy and protective", says Duffy, "and it seemed immovable. Harold Wilson tried to reform the civil service and failed totally." Similar hierarchies prevailed in the world of business and seemed to be particularly well entrenched in Britain.

Duffy, whose politics are far from Conservative, freely admits that the changes of the 1980s, the era of Reaganomics and Thatcherism, were "in some ways, catastrophic". The state ceased to be a protective force, while the virtues of competition and the market were trumpeted. Suddenly, the issue of space allocation became a matter not of tradition and custom but one subject to ruthless analysis in the cause of lower costs and greater competitiveness. Organisations which seemed set in their ways faced radical and rapid change.

In the last decade, DEGW has been active in promoting the transformation of such organisations, linking their new profiles to a new world of work which has cut British Telecom's (BT) workforce drastically, sent civil servants to greenfield sites and erased the last traces of the public service mentality from organisations like British Airways and the electricity and gas industries.

Even in their slimmed-down form, organisations of this sort are large and complex and it is their very scale which makes implementing change anything but easy. DEGW's long-running relationship with IBM, an organisation which showed a pioneering concern for new ways of working, helped form an approach which has since been applied to other large concerns. In Britain, Margaret Thatcher's privatisation crusade

The interior of 5 The Longwalk is now revealed as a dynamic example of late twentieth-century office architecture.

BT also occupies a building at Stockley Park designed by Arup Associates, original master-planners of the development with DEGW. This building, too, is laid out to a flexible open plan, with touchdown workstations supported by meeting rooms and interactive spaces.

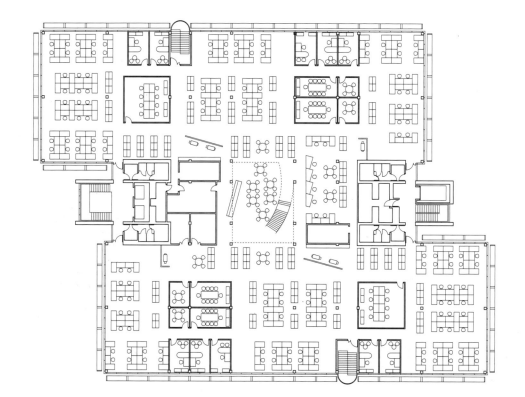

produced huge new private utilities – British Airways (BA), the British Airports Authority, British Telecom (BT) and British Gas, for example – run on entirely commercial lines.

Duffy's interest in the culture of organisations helped him understand the sociological changes which followed on from privatisation. BT, for example, was a huge and rambling company, with its sales and service staff based in a variety of small to medium-size offices – generally providing a second-rate office environment –

in city centres and suburbs. The Workstyle 2000 programme changed all that. It reflected the company's determination to prosper in a fiercely competitive international communications market. The older offices were scheduled for closure as the workforce was rapidly reduced from 170,000 to under 100,000. The entire BT estate was evaluated in terms of its future usefulness and its potential for sale or development.

One consequence of Workstyle 2000 was the decision to relocate staff from expensive, in-

convenient city-centre sites to the peripheries of cities. One such location, conveniently situated near Heathrow Airport and the M4 and M25 motorways, was Stockley Park. Together with Arup Associates, DEGW had been instrumental in masterplanning Stockley Park in the 1980s and was subsequently responsible for the space planning and fit-out of two of the buildings there – nos 4 and 5 The Longwalk. Acquired by BT in 1995, these were redesigned to house up to 3000 staff.

The principles behind BT's Stockley Park development were central to Workstyle 2000: mobility, flexibility, interaction. Open-plan work areas provide 'touchdown' desks for itinerant sales staff. The layout of workstations was designed to accommodate change over the years – DEGW always views buildings in terms of the relative longevity of their component parts. It was not just a matter of cutting property costs but also of giving staff the right kind of space necessary to maximise their potential. And the staff were managers of a new breed: highly mobile, motivated and involved in business worldwide. The approach to the redesign of the buildings had to reflect the character of the users.

The full-height foyer of 5 The Longwalk reveals the building as a complete entity.

There is a strong feeling of interaction in 5 The Longwalk: the café is close at hand for relaxation and the informal discussion of business.

Some BT staff are permanently based at Stockley Park. Many more spend only part of their working week there and need access to state-of-the-art work-stations as well as the chance to catch up with colleagues. The new office also provides a sense of place, itself a strong support for a highly mobile workforce.

27

BT recognised that an attractive café would be a vital element in the new office, a morale booster and an information exchange.

Informal spaces, where staff can share a coffee and work experiences, are an essential amenity in the new office.

The open-plan layout encourages discussion and communication and fosters teamwork. BT's Workstyle 2000 project was rooted in interaction and mobility, moving staff from a network of outdated city-centre offices to a number of new out-of-town sites, of which Stockley Park was a pioneering example.

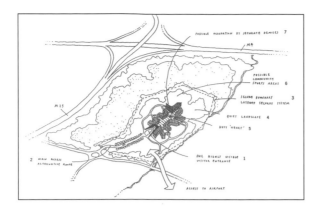

British Airways' Waterside headquarters is in an attractive landscaped park, close to Heathrow Airport and the M4 and M25 motorways.

British Airways, too, was rapidly and thoroughly modernised after privatisation, making it a very competitive leader in the world air travel market. Nicholas Grimshaw's Compass Centre, another striking building on the edge of Heathrow housing staff reporting facilities and operations control for the airline's fleet worldwide, was designed to break down the rigid caste divisions between flight deck and cabin crew in the interests of team working. It was revolutionary, but popular with staff. The facilities were vastly superior to those previously provided in buildings scattered around the airport. The Compass Centre, regarded by BA as an unqualified success, informed the briefing process undertaken by DEGW in respect of BA's new Waterside headquarters, which takes its cue, organisationally and architecturally, from a progressive European tradition of workplace design.

BA was a classic case of the determination to be 'firstest with the mostest'. As Duffy says, "the organisation could only press ahead with its mission to be a world leader. There was no way it could turn back into good old BEA and BOAC". The business case for Waterside – designed by Niels Torp – had to be clearly established. Everything about the new building should be an expression of the airline's business goals and objectives. The organisational brief produced by DEGW set benchmarks for success; every department was examined in detail and its work processes and patterns of time utilisation and space use analysed.

In the words of Sir Colin Marshall of BA, the central objective was to secure "a highly integrated unit responsible not only for

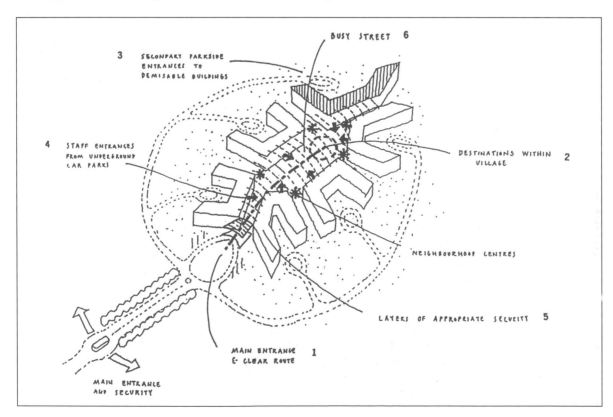

The layout, as developed in the brief by DEGW, is that of a 'village' with a main street at its centre, around which extend a series of working neighbourhoods.

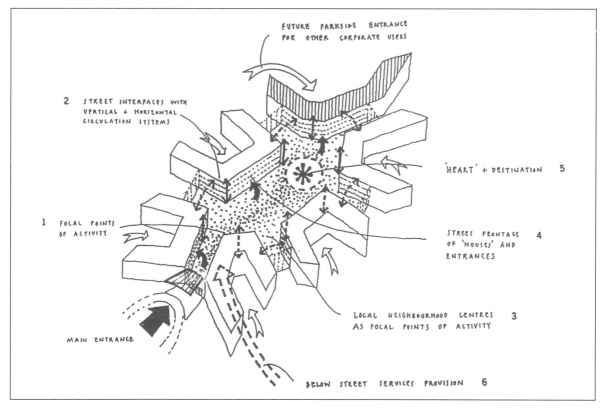

FUTURE PARKSIDE ENTRANCE
FOR OTHER CORPORATE USERS

2 STREET INTERFACES WITH
VERTICAL + HORIZONTAL
CIRCULATION SYSTEMS

'HEART' + DESTINATION 5

1 FOCAL POINTS
OF ACTIVITY

STREET FRONTAGE 4
OF 'HOUSES' AND
ENTRANCES

LOCAL NEIGHBOURHOOD CENTRES 3
AS FOCAL POINTS OF ACTIVITY

MAIN ENTRANCE

BELOW STREET SERVICES PROVISION 6

DEGW prepared a series of sketches for the architect Niels Torp which embodied the principles of a working village, the 'buildings' within it accommodating different functions but always encouraging a sense of community.

strategic decisions but also for 'hands on' management of an international business". The building at Waterside had to reflect this objective in its format and architectural vocabulary, though, of course, it also had to be a practical development, easily funded, which would represent a good investment.

DEGW's strategic brief developed the idea of a 'village', a metaphor which helped crystallise the physical elements which would make up the new headquarters. It would be a global village, but of human scale, with a mix of spaces

reflecting the great range of activity there: from intensive individual work, requiring calm and quiet, to networking and socialising.

Gradually a pattern of streets, neighbourhoods, lanes and houses emerged. Within this pattern there was a clear vision of change, an acceptance that, in the life of a building, services, fit-out and furnishings will change. The buildings themselves will be prestigious yet friendly in appearance, broken down into tangible working neighbourhoods but focused on a 'heart' where people would meet, talk and feel part of a dynamic whole.

BA was invited to back not just a building but a process of cultural business change. Teamwork, interaction, collaboration, group working, hands-on management and a total commitment to information technology were components. Waterside embodies BA's commitment to change, but it will also be a good place to work. As Colin Marshall put it, the company wanted a workplace "that attracts, retains and develops committed employees who share in the success of the company".

The DTI building was an unexceptional 1960s development, but it had potential for renewed life.

The human dimension of change is central to DEGW's work and is certainly a matter of concern to Francis Duffy. "In the past", he says, "you had a clear career structure. As you were promoted, you got more space, a private office. Now there are no fixed expectations. You must adapt or go under. There is a terrible logic to it all and this colours our view of society and life." Privatisation eroded the public domain and has had worrying consequences for some public services. But, in principle, Duffy accepts the rationale behind it: "It is based on a theory of value, relating spatial resources to needs, and has a design dimension that is not properly understood. The principle is beyond question, but it has to be made to work beneficially".

The era of privatisation has overturned established ways even in government and civil service circles, where bureaucracy, waste and inefficiency were often rampant and hierarchy was a way of life. A change in location may act as a catalyst for change but, more often, change has to take place on an existing site and within the confines of an existing building.

The headquarters of the Department of Trade and Industry (DTI) on Victoria Street, close to Westminster Abbey, was completed in 1962 and is one of a depressing progression of mundane post-war blocks along that thoroughfare. But, however unappealing its appearance, the building was basically sound and plannable and had a long life ahead of it; its deficiencies were mainly technical and environmental, together with a marked lack of good open-plan workspace. So marked were the failings of the building, indeed, that the DTI vacated it in 1991 to allow a radical refurbishment to extend its useful life.

DEGW were the architects and interior designers for the project, which also brought into play the practice's research and briefing skills. Involving the client is a key element in DEGW's strategy and the designs for the DTI were developed through a series of workshops which tackled every issue from the most fundamental to those which might seem trivial – for example, the location of tea points – but which matter to users. Though the project was necessarily fast-track – just three months from first concept to final scheme – the client was involved at every stage. (The DTI is unusual in government circles in having its own facilities management group.)

Reopened in 1995, the transformed DTI building accommodates 50 per cent more staff in vastly improved conditions. Superficially, it has been given a sleek

The DTI building's deficiencies were not structural but organisational. DEGW's overhaul provided vastly improved working conditions for 50 per cent more staff.

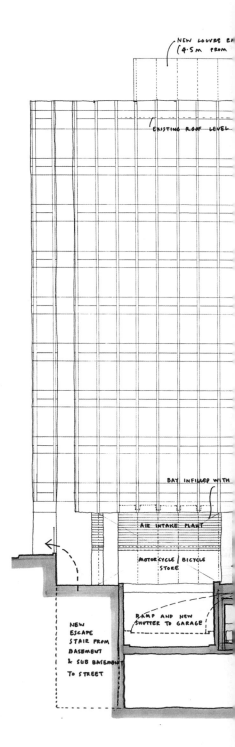

The exterior of the building to Victoria Street has been enlivened with an elegant new entrance pavilion.

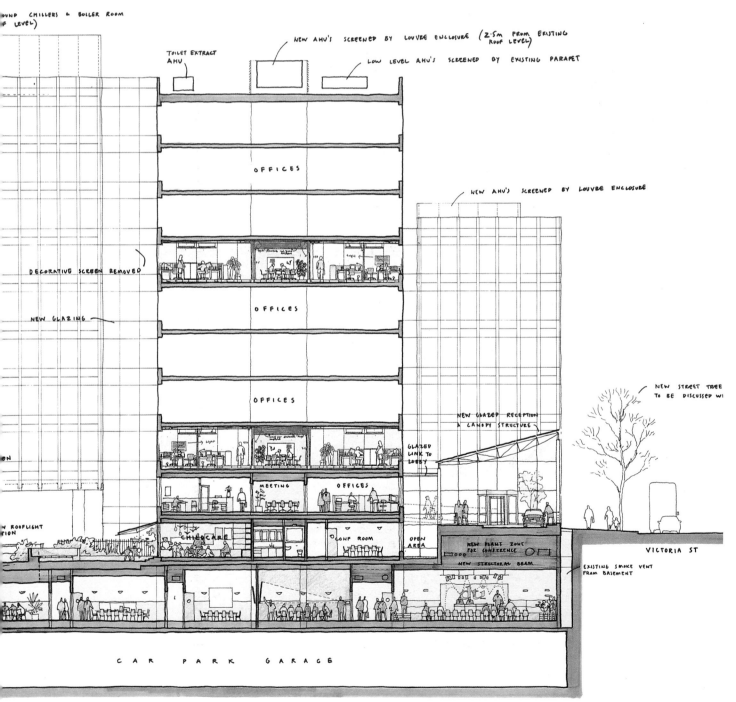

ROUND CHILLERS & BOILER ROOM
(F LEVEL)

TOILET EXTRACT AHU

NEW AHU'S SCREENED BY LOUVRE ENCLOSURE (2.5m FROM EXISTING ROOF LEVEL)

LOW LEVEL AHU'S SCREENED BY EXISTING PARAPET

OFFICES

NEW AHU'S SCREENED BY LOUVRE ENCLOSURE

DECORATIVE SCREEN REMOVED

OFFICES

NEW GLAZING

OFFICES

NEW STREET TREE TO BE DISCUSSED WI

NEW GLAZED RECEPTION & CANOPY STRUCTURE

GLAZED LINK TO LOBBY

MEETING   OFFICES

N ROOFLIGHT TION

CHILDCARE   CONF ROOM   OPEN AREA

NEW PLANT ZONE FOR CONFERENCE

VICTORIA ST

NEW STRUCTURAL BEAM

EXISTING SMOKE VENT FROM BASEMENT

CAR PARK GARAGE

Enhanced conference facilities, designed to serve the entire Whitehall community, were an important element in the DTI project.

Though structurally sound, '60s' office buildings tend to lack modern services and other amenities. DEGW's transformation of the DTI headquarters included the installation of raised floors for IT and chilled ceilings, as well as the reconfiguration of the workspaces, now open-plan but with plenty of support and private meeting rooms.

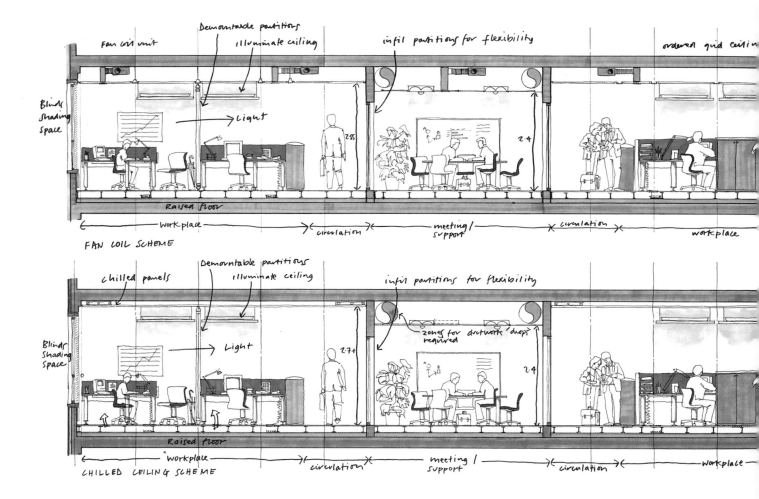

FAN COIL SCHEME

CHILLED CEILING SCHEME

The new floors are serviced to meet the needs of the next generation of civil servants.

The new foyer to the conference centre has been given an appropriate dignity which complements the functional character of the original architecture.

new look, notably by the addition of a new fully-glazed entrance pavilion. More significant, however, is the provision of a raised floor for cables and a new and more economic environmental control system based on the use of chilled ceilings. The spacious open-plan offices signal the arrival of the new office age in the civil service. The project is a typical DEGW product, merging theory and research about emerging user needs with skilful and imaginative practical execution.

Organisational change may be fuelled by the inexorable logic of economics and technology, producing a drive for efficiency and value for money, but this does not mean formula buildings designed to a uniform pattern. The organisation of the future will succeed because it is in tune with the needs of its staff and equipped to make optimum use of their abilities. This means buildings with a human dimension, designed for people who know what they want.

Informal meeting areas are provided in lobbies throughout the building.

The elegant new entrance pavilion provides access not only to the offices but also to the new conference facilities at basement level.

The staff restaurant, a popular destination with all who use the building, has a clear identity and presence.

The unusual configuration of the lifts, inherited from the original building, provides a dramatic entrance to each of the upper floors.

Though situated in the basement, the staff restaurant is flooded with daylight to create a distinctive space, ideal for socialising and relaxation, that brings the norms of corporate life to the civil service.

Spaces for informal meetings, over a tea or coffee break, are provided on all floors: the day of the civil service tea trolley is past.

37

Designed with engineers Waterman & Partners, the new entrance pavilion at the DTI building is a good example of DEGW's architectural philosophy: dynamic, elegant, and making use of modern materials and techniques to create a memorable, enjoyable space for the users.

Time

DEGW has always been fascinated by time as a critical dimension of architectural design. Its interest began very early in the 1970s with the realisation that, in office design, there is a huge difference between the quality of decision-making necessary to determine the architectural elements that concern the investor and the developer and those that satisfy the aspirations of the client and the tenant. The time horizon of the tenant tends to be measured in months; that of the developer, and certainly the investment institution, in decades. Somewhere between the building shell and the interior scenery lies the timescale of the design of environmental services – determined by developing user needs but also by the practical lifespan of the mechanical engineering components.

A new office concept for Scottish Enterprise explores the critical component of time in space.

In office design time matters a lot. Big, costly mistakes occur either when architects attempt to solve a 50-year problem with flimsy elements that can barely last five years or, even worse, when they attempt the opposite: to satisfy shifting, transient requirements with permanent or long-term architecture.

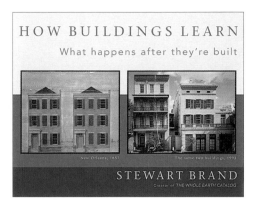

In his book, *How Buildings Learn*, Stewart Brand identified a fascination with permanence and transience as DEGW's chief characteristic.

Stewart Brand's diagram from *How Buildings Learn*: different components have different rates of change, often acting against each other.

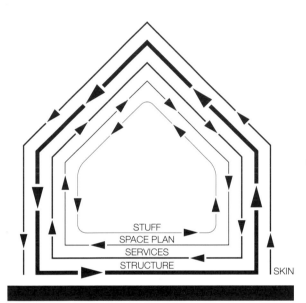

What difference has this continuing and fascinating distinction between permanence and transience made to DEGW's practice? Stewart Brand in his book, *How Buildings Learn*, sees it as DEGW's chief distinguishing characteristic. Certainly, a concern with time has deeply influenced DEGW's practice in consultancy and research – leading it, for example, to develop measures that rate buildings in terms of their capacity to accommodate change. Even more important to DEGW than the intellectual and practical implications of time on design, however, the imperative that drives the practice on, is the need to create an architectural aesthetic that combines permanence and transience and gives to each its due meaning and importance. Such an aesthetic will shape the twenty-first century.

Meanwhile, if DEGW's artistic ambitions were not stimulus enough, the practical, economic and operational concerns of its clients make the practice deeply and increasingly dissatisfied with the so-called timeless architecture that boxes it in so firmly. It is in conventional architectural practice that extreme versions of the denial of the existence of time are to be found. Many architects attempt to work as if buildings were eternal and as if time did not exist. Why should this be?

Lingering fragments of Modern Movement ideology – the powerful idea, for example, of *gestalt* which Gropius used to emphasise the totality of the building task – continue to provide some kind of intellectual underpinning for the persistent architectural habit of attempting to coin each new building as the complete, timeless expression of a single mind. Much could be said about the pervasive and generally malign influence of the Arts and Crafts Movement, still by far the strongest cultural factor in British architectural thought.

Ruskin and Morris's ideals led to increasingly forlorn attempts by individual architects to command, as master builders, the entire building process. It is chilling to see how Arts and Crafts, the Modern Movement, Neo-Rationalism, Classical Revivalism, the New Vernacular, Post-Modernism, Deconstructivism, all these passing architectural cults, share the same disregard for accommodating change, artistically, practically, or intellectually. It is depressing that each wave of fashion seems to mark yet another abdication by architects of control of some part of the building process. The underlying reason, as Marx would have been quick to point out, is economic.

What makes architects behave in the way they habitually do is not so much the way they are, nor how they are trained, nor what they believe, but the way they are paid. Architects' fees are still largely inseparable from the costs of building contracts, whether calculated as a

C. F. A. Voysey's 1906 office for the Essex and Suffolk Equitable Insurance Company, London: a classic of the Arts and Crafts Movement.

percentage of the contract sum, or as so many pounds or dollars per square metre or square foot. This, in turn, relates directly to how much power architects are capable of exerting on their clients and within the construction industry. The apparatus of an architect's appointment, building contracts, fee scales, plans of work, slowly accumulated over the last 150 years, has always tended in one direction only: towards the inevitable acceptance by architects of the one-off building as a conveniently packaged, complete and timeless entity. This is all simply, as the economists say, supply-side thinking.

In other words, architects have been captured by the industry they fondly imagine is their creature. Change is difficult and expensive to respond to and therefore it must, wherever possible, be eliminated.

The most practical people, for the most cost-effective but suboptimal reasons, sometimes end up behaving in the most absurd way. Anyone who has any acquaintance at all with the highly elaborated modes of procurement of buildings, particularly from the point of view of vulnerable, risk averse suppliers, must sympathise strongly with

the pressures which squeeze out the possibility of tolerating anything less than total control of the construction process. Enormous discipline is necessary to execute great building projects efficiently. Packages of information must be produced by the architect according to the strictest timetabling. Those parts of the client body closest to commissioning buildings are, in fact, even less tolerant of second thoughts and hesitation than the suppliers. They, too, are terrified of the disastrous financial consequences of a delayed, derailed, or disrupted building contract.

Such are the cogent reasons for attempting to freeze music, for getting it right on the night, for using buildings as a kind of strait-jacket to attempt to squash organisational change. Such also are the reasons for the nomadic, amnesiac and occasionally downright piratical behaviour of the building industry, forever moving on to seek new prizes, rarely looking back, never learning enough from experience, always restless, always avoiding contact with the real users – not the professional commissioners of buildings but those who suffer them in daily use, through time.

And how they suffer, those users! Not because anyone wants them to but because, if the priority of carrying out neat, self-contained building projects is asserted, as it usually is, it is impossible to reconcile atemporal neatness and self-containedness with the messy, unpredictable, open-ended, utterly time-dependent nature of modern commercial life.

The conflict between suboptimal, construction-based procedures in architecture and the totally different set of user-based priorities has always been obvious in office buildings. However, the rate of technological and organisational change has accelerated in the office in the last decade, perhaps more than in any other building type, and consequently the divergence between what is convenient to build and what is actually required has widened recently in a most spectacular way.

Which, of course, is the reason why, to cope with what have become intolerable pressures, new skills and procedures are being called into play. In office buildings themselves a quiet but inexorable shift is taking place from solving environmental problems by long-term architecture towards solving them with such short-term and easily replaceable elements as furniture. For three decades the clients' money, absolutely and

relatively, has been slipping away from traditional architecture. More positively, new methods for managing and designing for change are emerging. But these new design methods are very different from the way traditional architectural practice is conducted.

This context explains DEGW's special interest in the life cycle of buildings and its general desire, when starting out, to do exactly the opposite of what most conventional architectural practices were doing. Many of DEGW's most

Change over time is as applicable to the planning of cities, with their critically important trajectories of development, as it is to the planning of office space – ideas incorporated in this early DEGW masterplan for Enfield Island, north London.

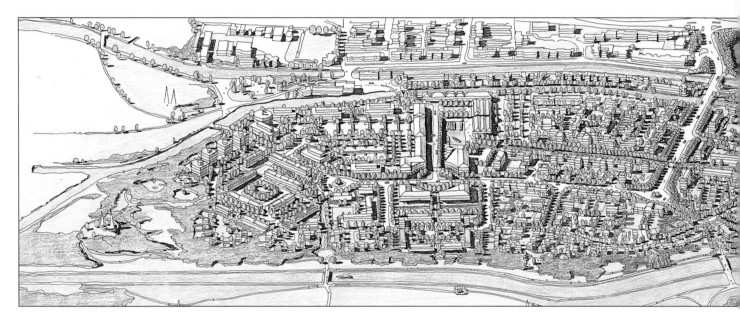

formative experiences were the direct outcome of studies in the United States in the 1960s. Systems thinking was in the air. To understand reality in terms of connections between social, political, economic and technological phenomena, within an environment of change, appealed particularly strongly to architects whose training inherently links things. To comprehend the big picture seemed more attractive than analytical modes of thinking, which tend to split and isolate variables to study them separately.

Two experiences at two very different scales opened the practice's eyes to the practical importance of time in design. The first was urban design. Cities are mankind's single largest artifacts. But change is inherent in them. They have very visible histories as well as critically important trajectories of development. Decline is always possible. The only way to comprehend the complex forces that shape cities is through studying their patterns of growth and change. The best way to change cities is to relate such changes to contemporary politics and economics.

The second experience lay at exactly the opposite scale – the micro-world of space planning as it was beginning to be practised in New York in the late '60s. There are many parallels with urban design. The interior design of offices involves many constituencies, many interest groups, often in conflict, all within the context of rigorous economic constraints and continuous change. The programming techniques that were developed by the newly founded, non-traditional design firms in New York at that time were very similar to the participative urban planning processes that were then being developed throughout the United States. The social, political, economic and, indeed, technological issues are iden-

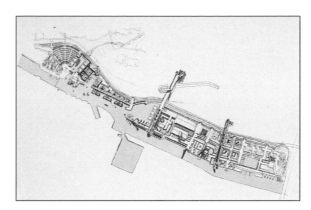

An early DEGW proposal for the mixed-use re-development of York Quay, on the Clyde waterfront in Glasgow.

A detail view of the Rummelsburgerbucht masterplan, Berlin, showing the landmark 'square' by the lake.

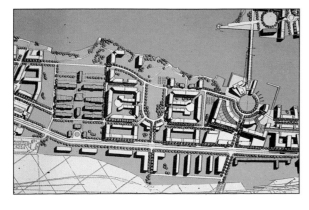

tical, in fact, except for the more intimate scale of application.

What both urban designers and space planners had discovered – and what DEGW quickly learned – is that the unit of analysis by which an architectural practice should be organised and planned is not the capacity to deliver a single or even a series of isolated projects but, instead, the ability to develop and sustain ongoing relations with clients who are never unitary, always developing and continually changing. Just as urban designers look at the systemic, organic, reality of a total neighbourhood or an entire city so space planners, at their best, think in terms of the changing organisations, often in multiple buildings, always redrawing their boundaries, always rethinking their ways of working. Time is the critical variable at both scales of planning for change.

The practical consequences of this time-based approach to office design have been immense. In the micro-world of an office's interior design, it makes an enormous difference if both designers and users understand that some architectural elements are relatively long-term and difficult to change, while others are far more ephemeral and can respond instantly to shifts in the pattern of demand. This insight, common enough in interior design practice in New York in the '60s, was formally articulated by DEGW in the early 1970s as the 'shell, services, scenery, settings' model, each of these elements having a different lifespan and each needing to be designed with a high degree of independence from the others, so that different cycles of intervention and replacement can be more easily reconciled.

This notion horrified many conventional architects because it was seen, quite wrongly, to

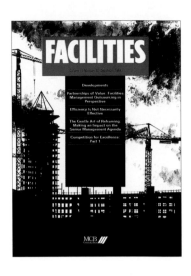

DEGW established *Facilities* in 1983, in anticipation of the rise of the facilities management profession.

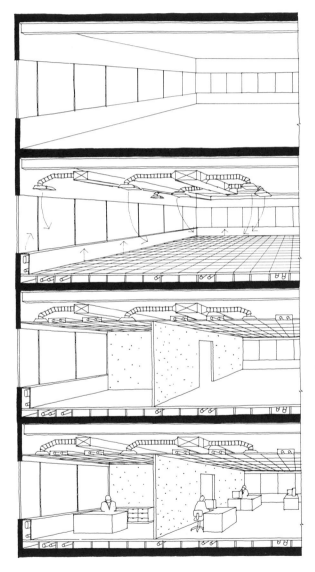

Shell, services, scenery, setting – the different layers of the modern office each have their own life cycle which must be incorporated into the final design.

legitimise a further loss of architectural control and, worse, because it opened the door to design intervention by the users themselves. No wonder DEGW embraced Herman Hertzberger's Centraal Beheer (1974) as an eloquent architectural exposition of the aesthetic potential of the interplay between the long- and the short-term, between design by the architect and by the end-user, between the high art of architecture and the taste of ordinary people.

Awareness of time and the importance of managing office space through time made DEGW very conscious of the need for an architectural equivalent to software – using an obvious comparison with the world of computers – which could be used to extract maximum value over time from the hardware of office design. Hence the practice's enthusiastic support in the early '80s for facilities management, which it saw as providing the potential for entirely necessary managerial software that could complement the hardware of office design.

DEGW helped to establish what is now the flourishing British Institute of Facilities Management (BIFM). In 1983, shortly after publishing the summary of the results of the first ORBIT study, the practice founded the newsletter *Facilities* – which still continues – because it correctly anticipated that facilities management would be given a tremendous boost by the necessity of managing the physical consequences of distributed intelligence in the office.

Nothing, as the psychologist Kurt Lewin once said, is as practical as a good theory. All professions exist to open up options for the future and all depend upon the development of organised bodies of knowledge. Much of DEGW's research, as well as the best of its design work, since the early 1980s has been in developing the theoretical basis for the future of architecture, facilities management and urban design. Much of this work has been about the changing relationships between cities and people and buildings and organisations. In other words, for almost two decades, DEGW's research effort has essentially been focused on designing with time in mind.

The two ORBIT studies on the impact of information technology (IT) on office buildings carried out in the UK and USA (1981/82 and 1985 respectively) tackled what are still the key issues in office design: the direct and indirect effects of IT on the use of physical resources by organisations. The ORBIT work has since led to a whole series of further research studies, all sup-

ported in the same multi-client way, all addressing the same shifting and changing relationship between the physical and the organisational, and all increasingly concerned with time as a variable in the effective design and management of office

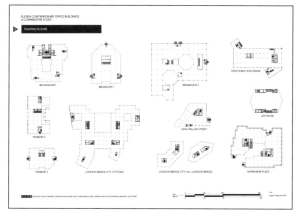

The comparative appraisal of building performance was first pioneered by DEGW during early studies for the Broadgate project.

space. Over this period of development, time has become more and more important for DEGW's understanding of the field.

The three main practical consequences of the ORBIT studies are, first, the development of systematic methods to measure the capacity of buildings to accommodate change; second, an increasing reliance on sectoral studies of the development of client requirements to both validate and calibrate such measurements of building capacity; and third, the development of time-based models which are intended to explain, in as elegant a way as possible, the likely consequences of change.

Let us take each of these facets of DEGW's developing methodology in turn. The measurement of the capacity of buildings to accommodate change was initiated in ORBIT 1, but was made fully operational in the development of

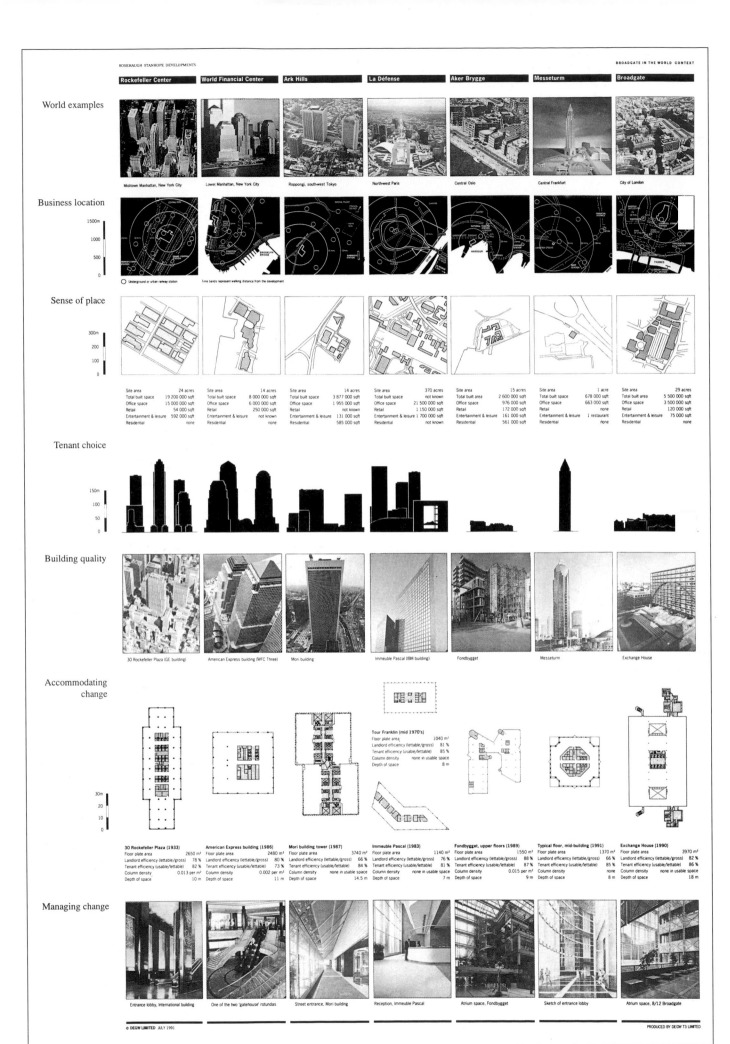

	Rockefeller Center	World Financial Center	Ark Hills	La Défense	Aker Brygge	Messeturm	Broadgate
World examples	Mid-town Manhattan, New York City	Lower Manhattan, New York City	Roppongi, south-west Tokyo	Northwest Paris	Central Oslo	Central Frankfurt	City of London

Business location — Underground or urban railway station. Time bands represent walking distance from the development

Sense of place

	Rockefeller Center	World Financial Center	Ark Hills	La Défense	Aker Brygge	Messeturm	Broadgate
Site area	24 acres	14 acres	14 acres	370 acres	15 acres	1 acre	29 acres
Total built space	19 200 000 sqft	8 000 000 sqft	3 877 000 sqft	not known	2 600 000 sqft	678 000 sqft	5 500 000 sqft
Office space	15 000 000 sqft	6 000 000 sqft	1 955 000 sqft	21 500 000 sqft	976 000 sqft	663 000 sqft	3 500 000 sqft
Retail	54 000 sqft	250 000 sqft	not known	1 150 000 sqft	172 000 sqft	none	120 000 sqft
Entertainment & leisure	592 000 sqft	not known	131 000 sqft	1 700 000 sqft	161 000 sqft	1 restaurant	75 000 sqft
Residential	none	none	585 000 sqft	not known	561 000 sqft	none	none

Tenant choice

Building quality

30 Rockefeller Plaza (GE building)	American Express building (WFC Three)	Mori building	Immeuble Pascal (IBM building)	Fondbygget	Messeturm	Exchange House

Accommodating change

Tour Franklin (mid 1970's)
Floor plate area 1040 m²
Landlord efficiency (lettable/gross) 81 %
Tenant efficiency (usable/lettable) 85 %
Column density none in usable space
Depth of space 8 m

	30 Rockefeller Plaza (1933)	American Express building (1986)	Mori building tower (1987)	Immeuble Pascal (1983)	Fondbygget, upper floors (1989)	Typical floor, mid-building (1991)	Exchange House (1990)
Floor plate area	2650 m²	2480 m²	3740 m²	1140 m²	1550 m²	1370 m²	3970 m²
Landlord efficiency (lettable/gross)	78 %	80 %	66 %	76 %	88 %	66 %	82 %
Tenant efficiency (usable/lettable)	82 %	73 %	84 %	81 %	87 %	85 %	86 %
Column density	0.013 per m²	0.002 per m²	none in usable space	none in usable space	0.015 per m²	none	none in usable space
Depth of space	10 m	11 m	14.5 m	7 m	9 m	8 m	18 m

Managing change

Entrance lobby, International building	One of the two 'gatehouse' rotundas	Street entrance, Mori building	Reception, immeuble Pascal	Atrium space, Fondbygget	Sketch of entrance lobby	Atrium space, 8/12 Broadgate

© DEGW LIMITED JULY 1991

PRODUCED BY DEGW T3 LIMITED

the Building Appraisal techniques which analyse and compare the configuration of whole buildings, floorplates and servicing systems with regard to specific user requirements and different commercial sectors – banks, the insurance industry, law firms and so on. The typical result of a building appraisal exercise on an existing or a proposed building is a relative rating against other buildings which quite deliberately resembles an assessment of a white goods product in the consumer magazine *Which*. If a building has the capacity to accommodate several predefined profiles, it has, by extrapolation, the ability to accommodate a lot of change.

Building appraisal played an important role during the development of building specifications for Broadgate and Stockley Park, as well as many other development projects, and the technique's validity has subsequently been tested successfully in a series of hard-fought valuation arbitrations in which the method has been used to determine the ongoing 'use value' of a number of office buildings. Building appraisal techniques have also been developed in a series of studies of so-called 'building intelligence', defined by DEGW as the capacity of a building to benefit the people it houses, both as an environmentally responsive mechanism and as an aid in achieving the social or business objectives of the client.

Two such studies have been completed, *The Intelligent Building in Europe* (1993) and *Intelligent Buildings in South East Asia* (1996). A third in the series, *Intelligent Buildings in Latin America*, will be completed in 1998. Clearly, building appraisal, in its continually developing forms, remains a vital part of DEGW's tool box

of methodologies and, naturally, plays an important and informative role in the practice's own design work.

'Future proofing' is a shorthand way of describing what building appraisal does for an investor's portfolio, for a developer's project or for a user-client's outline project. Building appraisal has the advantage of both modelling and testing the impact of change on office buildings. However, by its very nature, building appraisal depends upon the accurate predictions of organisational change, presented in such a way that the impact of change upon architectural variables is made evident in a systematic and comparative way.

	Bürolandschaft offices	Traditional British speculative offices	New 'Broadgate' type of British speculative office	Traditional North American speculative office	The new North European office
No. of storeys	5	10	10	80	5
Typical floor size	2,000sqm	1,000sqm	3,000sqm	3,000sqm	Multiples of 2,000sqm
Typical office depth	40m	13.5m	18m and 12m	18m	10m
Furthest distance from perimeter aspect	20m	7m	9-12m	18m	5m
Efficiency: net to gross		80%	85%	90%	70% (lots of public circulation)
Maximum cellularization (% of usable)	20%	70%	40%	20%	80%
Type of core	Semi-dispersed	Semi-dispersed	Concentrated: extremely compact	Concentrated: extremely compact	Dispersed: stairs more prominent than lifts
Type of HVAC services	Centralized	Minimal	Floor by floor	Centralized	Decentralized: minimal use of HVAC

Different types of office and how they measure up: appraisal of building performance is part of DEGW's concern to 'future-proof' developer projects.

DEGW has made important advances in this difficult area of research: first, through continually upgraded studies of user opinion, user priorities and user expectations in various sectors of our clients' activities; and second, through modelling the more general impact of changes in

Below: a diagram from *The Responsible Workplace*, showing the tension between an organisation's need to minimise costs while simultaneously adding value at different levels of decision-making.

Differentiation

low   high

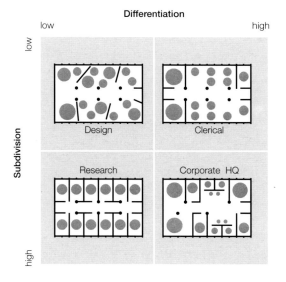

Francis Duffy's doctoral thesis at Princeton established early models which began to explore the relationship between office layout and types of organisation.

IT on organisations and, subsequently, upon the design of buildings. Two notable studies of this more general kind are *The Responsible Workplace* (1993) and *New Environments for Working* (1998). The first of these examined how the combination of environmental and economic concerns was likely to affect office design, while the second examined what impact new ways of using office time and office space would have upon certain standard specifications which are based on static – and thus incorrect – assumptions of how people use office buildings over time.

The most complete exposition of DEGW's sectoral approach to change is found in *The Changing City* (1989), which was an examination of change in seven sectors of the economy of the City of London. The most challenging critique of the assumptions which lie behind conventional office design is undoubtedly *New Environments for Working*. Together they make a formidable attack upon conventional supply-side thinking in design and construction. From a scientific and

methodological point of view, such studies are unusual in that they do not simply describe what is, nor do they limit themselves to the impact of change on single, isolated variables. Instead, the practice's technique is deliberately synoptic, open-ended, future-seeking and value-laden – consequences of the architects' design training which treats buildings and their users as a systemic whole.

DEGW's continuing interest in time has led inexorably towards the development of models that not only summarise what has been learned from building appraisal and sectoral studies about the impact of change on office design, but which are also deliberately intended to predict what emerging patterns of change are likely to mean for the design of future buildings and for future ways of procuring and managing them.

The history of these models goes back to Francis Duffy's earlier studies at Princeton, in 1969, where a two-dimensional model was first used to categorise different types of office layout and organisational structure and, most importantly, to explore the relationship between layout and

Minimising Cost

Location and the city

Procurement and tenure

Building intelligence

Recycling and re-use

Building shell

Building skin

Services and the internal environment

Layout: openness and enclosure

Furniture and settings

Facilities management

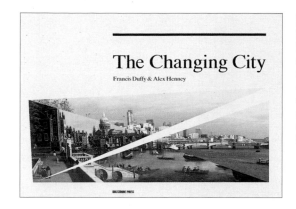

organisation. The weakness of the Princeton work was that change was not given enough prominence. Later DEGW models, and especially those prepared in the course of the development of ORBIT 2 (1985) and of 'Workplace Envisioning' with Steelcase (1991 to 1995), all stress the importance of the time dimension and of predicting the direction of organisational change.

To illustrate how important change has become in DEGW's current thinking, consider the model first developed in *The Responsible Workplace* (1993). This is based on the idea that, when planning their spatial strategies, all organisations must obey two imperatives: to drive down occupancy costs, and to add value to their operations by encouraging and stimulating the workforce. Each is generally thought to be diametrically opposed to the other. However, because the model is dynamic, it can be demonstrated that both imperatives can be reconciled in various ways: different pressures on each axis bring, at any one point of time, different degrees of reconciliation; and a general trajectory of change is predicted.

Three versions of this model demonstrate its versatility. The original *Responsible Workplace* model used the juxtaposition of the two axes, adding value and driving down costs, to argue how innovation in the specification of design hardware and facilities management software could be expected to accommodate new ways of working – initially simple improvements in facilities management, ultimately radical and far-reaching changes in the structuring of cities. The second version is used as a means of predicting how the allocation of space by organisations is likely to develop from unpressured reliance on grade and status, through an increasing emphasis on functionality, to the eventual and inevitable redesign of all work processes.

The same dynamic is used in the third version to explain managerial processes. Currently, in many organisations it is possible to tolerate the totally separate management of human resources, IT and buildings. Under increasing pressure to drive down costs and simultaneously to add value, all organisations are likely to co-ordinate these managerial functions at first, and eventually to combine them to achieve, under extreme competitive pressure, maximum strategic impetus.

This is only one example of the increasing

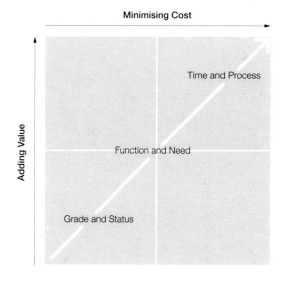

determination of DEGW, in both consultancy and design, to articulate ideas about how to push change to the top of the agenda and to make sure that urban design, space planning and facilities management initiatives are correlated with strategic business and social issues. Such studies can only be carried out in the context of practice because it is only there that the questions are relevant, the data is accessible and the urgency to act is sufficiently acute.

Data about buildings in use through time has become critical to accelerate change. DEGW has given considerable attention to the development of techniques of observation and measurement. Increasingly, the emphasis has been on studying the use of space through time because this is where the best clues are about how to put buildings to more effective as well as more efficient use. Hence DEGW's 'Time Utilisation Survey', a computerised means of measuring where people are in the office and what they are doing – absolutely critical data if the potential of 'desk-sharing' and wider, richer and more supportive work settings can be justified. Hence DEGW's development of the 'Workplace Performance' measures that allow users to state their priorities for change. Hence DEGW's continuing commitment – after almost 30 years of experience – to 'post-occupancy evaluation', systematically completing the loop between building design and building use: 'feeding forward' as Thomas Markus so acutely described the process.

All such techniques become cumulatively more valuable as comparative data builds up. One activity of DEGW that has become more and more important at both urban and building scales is brief writing – a skill that is based on ever-accumulating experience of how cities and buildings can best be designed to accommodate change over time. DEGW has always worked with other architects – helping them to explore, articulate and comprehend changing client requirements – and the development of an accurate and imaginative brief is often the best way to identify those demands, while at the same time building up the profession's knowledge base. A good brief is particularly important in architectural competitions and in preparing projects of a special or innovative kind.

DEGW values brief writing because it represents another order of design skill – different from and supplementary to project design skills. The chief contribution of the brief writer, apart from interpreting client needs, is to be able to see each particular, one-off project in terms of historical precedent, in the light of similar con-

Time utilisation surveys measure precise patterns of occupation and activity in the office, so that workplace design can be matched to use.

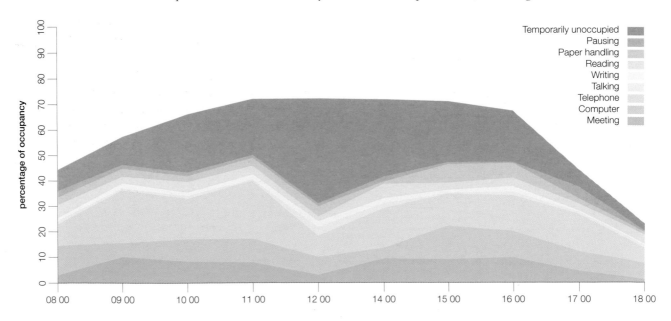

'Hot-desking' at the Tokyo office of the Japanese furniture company Kokuyo: new technology means sharing space and time.

temporary initiatives and in the context of probable future changes in client requirements. Properly conducted, brief writing introduces a statistical, probabilistic, risk-management perspective to design. Above all, brief writing reminds designers of what they so often underplay and even sometimes entirely omit from serious consideration, the dimension of time.

Brief writing is a form of design that is particularly relevant to DEGW's overall intellectual and artistic programme because the briefing process raises so many issues to do with the fragile relation between increasingly transient user requirements and relatively permanent building forms. However, DEGW is interested in many aspects and many modes of design. What buildings and interiors look like matters enormously.

That the practice is also interested in the design process, in facilities management, in how buildings are used over time, in what buildings are for, in brief writing and programming, by no means releases DEGW as architects and designers from its obligation to design world-class buildings and the finest possible interiors. Rather the opposite: the practice's ability to talk abstractly about design as consultants is inextricably linked to its ability to achieve excellence in the design of built projects – and vice versa. Each kind of skill tests and validates the other.

Designing for change over time should be stimulating rather than constraining for designers. Architects ought to enjoy the constant, demand-led renegotiations that are inevitable when many diverse constituencies involve themselves not just in the design process but equally in the re-invention of the use of space over time. DEGW believes that clients, as they change, will become more discriminating, more demanding, in other words will follow the logic of the models of

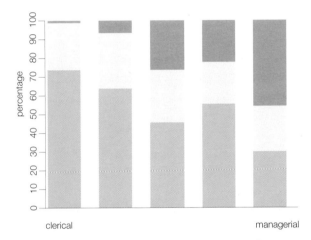

As this space utilisation survey for a North American insurance company demonstrates, good design depends on the best data.

change described earlier. They will demand far more supple and imaginative responses from architects. They will not be satisfied with rigid, centralised, top-down ways of delivering the built environment. They will want to share ownership of design so that the boundary between designer and designed-for will become far less distinct. They will spend less on long-term architecture and more on transient things. Such challenges are not bad. They stimulate invention.

The work that is illustrated in this book is diverse and varied, but not eclectic. What all the projects have in common is the search for appropriate forms to accommodate the thoughtful, demanding, changing people that will use them. The logic that has generated each project and each intellectual departure – environmental, social, the distribution of services, the accommodation of different requirements over time – is always evident. Each one of these DEGW designs has been driven by ideas. And of all the ideas that have obsessed DEGW over the years and have shaped its work, none has been more influential than what the concept of time means for design.

Strategic Briefing

A new building has its origins in the perceived need of a user or group of users for space. A company or institution may be driven by the simple need for more space or – and this is increasingly the case – for a different sort of space, reflecting new ways of working. For a developer, the key issue is creating the space that will let, space that reflects the current and future requirements of the users who are envisaged as occupiers. Strategic briefing, as one of DEGW's core areas of expertise, is a vital stage in the development and commissioning process. A building operates on many levels, aesthetic and practical, public and private, but, increasingly, buildings need to be seen not just in space, as physical objects, but also in time, as organisms which have a lifespan during which they will inevitably change and adapt.

According to Colin Cave, former chief executive and now a consultant at DEGW, strategic briefing is about "envisaging how buildings are going to be used. It is a matter of identifying strategic requirements, describing possible solutions and setting the critical success factors for a project, together with the means of measuring or calibrating success". Strategic briefing, in short, asks the difficult question: what is a good development? By considering a

DEGW's strategic study for the MoD's Procurement Executive headquarters, at Abbey Wood, produced a detailed brief for the site. The idea of clusters of buildings around a central 'high street' was fundamental. Interaction and integration were high priorities.

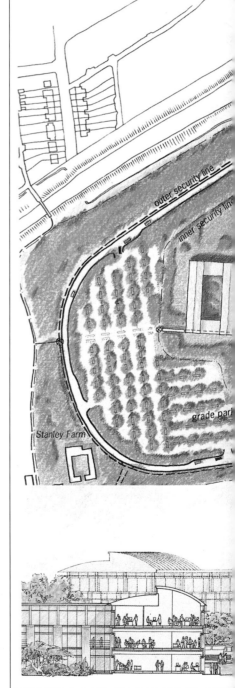

Abbey Wood, seen here in its final form, was conceived as a campus of inter-related buildings that included many common facilities, such as the library shown here.

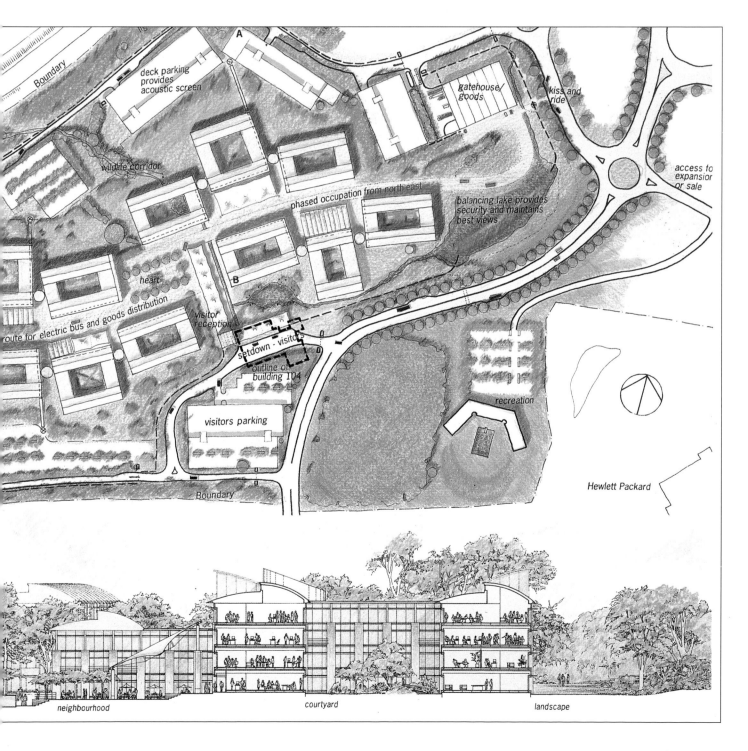

Boundary

deck parking provides acoustic screen

wildlife corridor

gatehouse/ goods

kiss and ride

phased occupation from north-east

balancing lake provides security and maintains best views

access to expansion or sale

heart

B

route for electric bus and goods distribution

visitor reception

setdown - visitors

outline of building 104

visitors parking

recreation

Boundary

Hewlett Packard

neighbourhood

courtyard

landscape

55

As developed by the architects Percy Thomas Partnership, the buildings at Abbey Wood have been designed to the standards of the commercial world.

project in a broad, synoptic context – which encompasses the underlying business issues and the 'culture' of the institution promoting the project – it informs and guides the development and design process. Strategic briefing is not to be confused with the detailed briefing process nor with the tactical programming of a project: it precedes and assists and, indeed, transcends both.

Developing buildings is big business, costly and risky – and ruinous if the formula is wrong. It is a matter of supply and demand, a central idea in strategic briefing. A business case has to be expressed in bricks and mortar or, more likely, steel and glass. Supply and demand are conventionally depicted as two intersecting lines; in a building project, supply is about

the intended space provision and demand is a matter of what the promoters are trying to achieve. The point where they meet is critical. But it is often hard, in Colin Cave's words, for an organisation "to get out of the wood so it can see the trees".

DEGW seeks to establish objective criteria for judging a project. For Cave, "the good strategic brief hovers between description and prescription". It is about "setting the language" for a project and hence the character of the architectural envelope and the space it contains. Consequently, a building can end up as something very different from the initial vision of a client. Central to DEGW's architecture of change is the involvement of users in developing a real understanding of what a building does

and of its potential for accommodating change.

Prescription, predictably, is seen as anti-innovation; it describes those elements in a strategic brief which are set, immovable. When DEGW worked, for example, with the Ministry of Defence (MoD) on several major projects, tight security was a prescribed factor which could not be dispensed with. In an ideal world, a strategic brief would be based on a description of needs, with an openness to all possible solutions and an overriding emphasis on performance.

The MoD, however, does provide a good example of an organisation whose accommodation needs had to be considered in the context of rapid organisational change. Traditionally conservative and dominated by the rigid divi-

DEGW's original masterplan proposed interconnected groups of buildings to form semi-independent neighbourhoods in a landscaped and largely pedestrianised park.

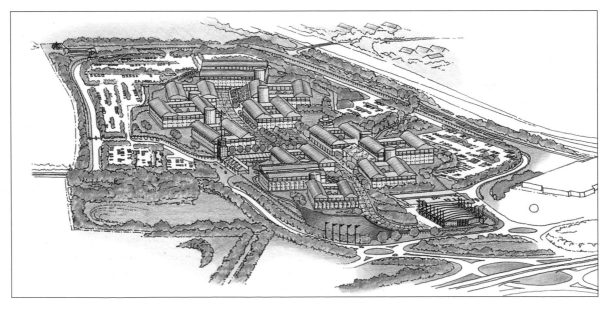

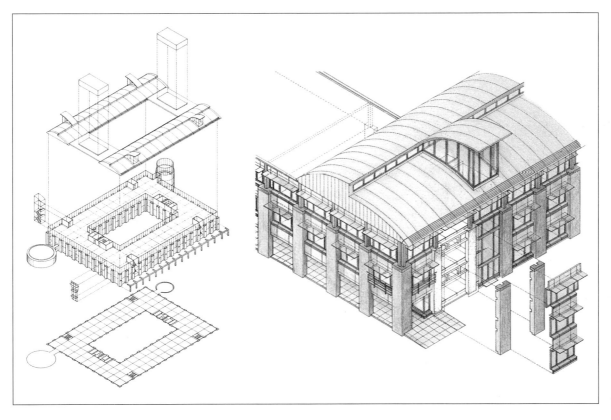

DEGW's briefing diagrams indicated narrow floorplates that allowed ample daylight to penetrate the offices. The buildings are designed for high energy efficiency, and include a relatively high proportion of masonry to glazing in the facades and active sun screening.

sions between the three armed services, the Ministry had to respond to steadily increased pressure for economy and greater efficiency. The new MoD office development at Abbey Wood, Bristol, was rooted in the concept of 'purpling' – purple being the colour that results from a mix of RAF grey, navy blue and army khaki.

Abbey Wood was to house 5000 staff from the MoD's Procurement Executive. It was clear that a very large area of new buildings – eventually over 1.5 million square feet of space – would be required, but DEGW's initial im-

pression, when appointed in 1992 to prepare a strategic study, was that "the MoD was construction-oriented, not business change oriented". Old ways die hard and the 'purpling' process was still contentious. Clearly, one way to advance it was through the provision of interchangeable neighbourhoods on the new site in place of the strictly defined territories of the past, now seen as wasteful and a hindrance to good management.

The new management and organisational structure had to be expressed in the format of the

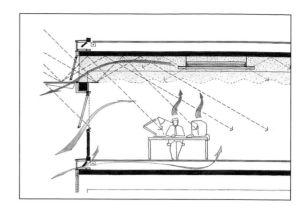

The internal character of the completed buildings incorporates the ideas of DEGW's basic strategy, a user-oriented layout, where working areas are close to interactive spaces, arranged around internal 'streets'.

offices. And from that point, the layout of the site and the nature of the architecture would emerge.

Getting the basic strategy right is the starting point. In the case of Abbey Wood, DEGW's strategic study, strongly endorsed by the MoD, was followed by a commission to produce a brief for the site, buildings, infrastructure and logistics. DEGW subsequently became part of the team, led by Bovis Project Management, which undertook the execution of the brief. The 12 buildings (eventually designed by Percy Thomas Partnership) are arranged in neighbourhood 'clusters', with a central square and pedestrian spine or 'high street'.

The layout was very specific to the needs of the users and reflects DEGW's passionate belief in using workplace design to support organisational change. From the initial workshops set up to determine the needs of staff to the close collaboration of all members of the project team in implementing the brief – landscape design, for example, was seen as a vital ingredient not an afterthought – the project was characterised by a strongly synoptic approach and a belief in designing in time as well as in space. The process of change is still at work in the MoD – hence DEGW's recent commission to produce a strategic brief for the Ministry's Whitehall headquarters.

Left: DEGW proposed that the cooling and ventilation requirements be satisfied using fresh air ducts at floor level, extracting through high-level windows.

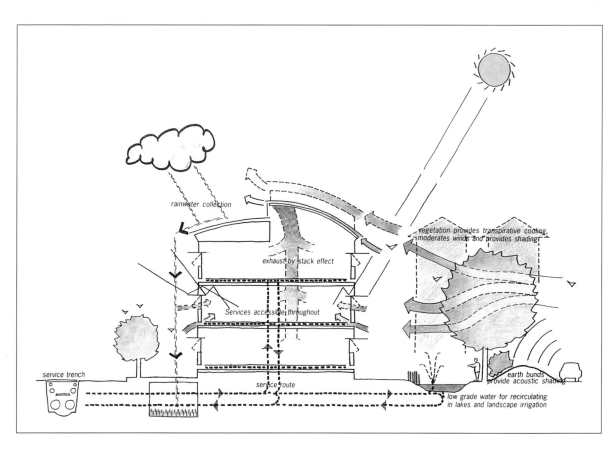

rainwater collection

vegetation provides transpirative cooling, moderates winds and provides shading

exhaust by stack effect

Services accessible throughout

service trench

service route

earth bunds provide acoustic shading

low grade water for recirculating in lakes and landscape irrigation

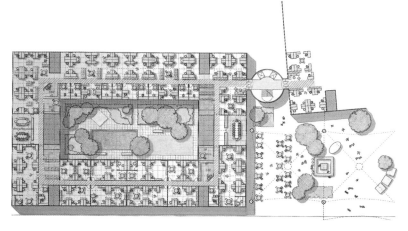

A low-energy design was central to DEGW's proposals. Air-conditioning was ruled out from the start on the grounds of high capital and running costs. Sun shading, opening windows and the use of cross ventilation provided a 'natural' solution to servicing issues.

The Abbey Wood buildings are open-plan and represent a new departure for the Ministry.

Percy Thomas Partnership's completed development at Abbey Wood is faithful to the concept of a campus in a landscaped park. The landscaping is more than ornamental: it creates a healthy microclimate near the buildings, while the lake provides a more attractive barrier than old-style MoD fencing.

The finished buildings provide open-plan office space suitable for group working, with meeting spaces always close at hand.

By the end of the 1980s working conditions within the Prudential's much-loved landmark on High Holborn were completely outdated.

Strategic briefing can be seen as the oil that lubricates the wheels of change. Very large and long-established companies can foster conservative attitudes to the workplace, and the relationship between an organisation and a building or site it has occupied over a long period can be an impediment to change. Prudential Assurance had occupied its High Holborn headquarters, a handsome Gothic Revival building by Alfred Waterhouse, for over a century before DEGW was called in, in 1989, to advise on a radical restructuring of both the organisation and the building.

"Supply and demand analysis was central to the 'Pru' project", says Colin Cave. The core Victorian buildings on the site were listed Grade II*, but there were later additions regarded as dispensable and providing scope for greatly increased space provision. The Prudential was being rationalised in the aftermath of the City's 'Big Bang'. The headquarters was a clear asset, on a wonderful site, but it was inefficiently utilised and the internal arrangements of the buildings were not propitious to the new, more interactive ways of working. Change was essential.

The company's own portfolio management department was the client for the restructured complex, but its facilities managers were charged with delivering the product and it was to the latter that DEGW reported. They had a clear idea of what they wanted and how much they were prepared to pay. DEGW's brief was both organisational and architectural; the practice was commissioned to advise and to refurbish the interiors of the retained Victorian buildings, combining their nineteenth-century vigour with twenty-first century organisational methods.

DEGW's brief combined the conservation of the existing listed building with an innovative approach to the use of space within.

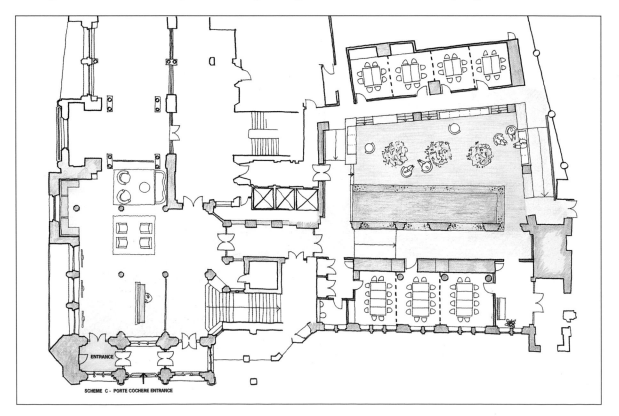

SCHEME C - PORTE COCHERE ENTRANCE

ENTRANCE

New atria were formed out of existing spaces between the Victorian buildings, providing interesting contrasts between old and new.

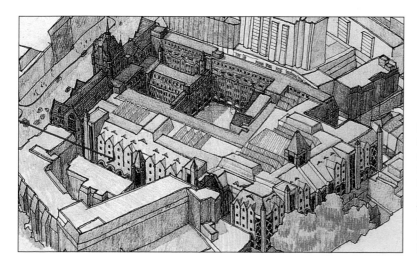

Up to two-thirds of the extended complex, either refurbished or reconstructed, could be let after the Prudential's own space requirements had been assessed.

Two new atria were formed in the West Court section of the complex, retained by Prudential for its own use and reconstructed by DEGW.

Well-furnished meeting rooms have been provided throughout the renovated buildings.

New furnishings, including a state-of-the-art conference table, have given the historic boardroom a new lease of life.

There is a new restaurant *(left)* in the basement, a vital amenity and furnished in entirely contemporary style. In contrast, the typical office areas *(far left)* combine modern fit-out and equipment with elements of the Grade II*-listed building, a juxtaposition which adds visual interest and emphasises the standing of the company.

65

Office interiors in the original building were subdivided by handsome but rather oppressive partitions, a layout which was not popular with staff.

In 1994, Boots the Chemists decided its listed D90 building needed to expand in line with the growth of the company.

Boots the Chemists is another household name among British businesses. Its large office and factory complex on the edge of Nottingham contains some remarkably innovative buildings, including the 1930s production blocks designed by Owen Williams. Then as now, change was driven by technological advances. In recent decades, the office building has undergone changes as revolutionary as those of the Industrial Revolution. Office architecture, in the words of DEGW's David Jenkin, has to "come out of real, practical needs, not preconceived stylistic devices. The right space for the right use is what is needed".

DEGW's interest in typologies – traditionally a system of strict classification – reflects its commitment to change. The office has a

typology of its own: variations in layout strictly mirror variations in ways of working and this analysis is itself a formula for change and the emergence of interactive, user-directed workspaces.

One of the most handsome of the buildings on the Boots 'campus' is the head office block, D90, completed in 1967 to designs by the American practice Skidmore, Owings & Merrill. Admired for its cool Miesian aesthetic – it is now a listed building – D90 had become inadequate not only in size but in terms of technology and a dated internal layout, with substantial areas of partitioned cellular offices.

DEGW's approach to the transformation of the headquarters block – a radical, though sensitive, refurbishment with the construc-

tion of a new, linked addition – emerged from a strategic briefing process which included thorough analysis of users' needs and a detailed financial assessment which together formed the business case for the project. Understanding the culture of the company was a key priority from the start. The company valued its traditions, but wanted to ensure its place in the competitive market of the future. Briefing and design were integrated in achieving the right sort of interactive space needed for a dynamic twenty-first century organisation. Boots the Chemists provides an excellent example of DEGW's holistic approach to researching and redesigning the workplace.

But the starting point is always an understanding of practical and

The D90 building had to change, but there was universal agreement that the elegance of its architecture – designed in 1967 by Skidmore, Owings & Merrill – should not be compromised in the updating process.

organisational needs. Sometimes, the analysis can produce surprising results. Cambridge University envisaged a new building being added to the 'Raised Faculty' complex, designed by Casson Conder in the 1960s. Space seemed to be limited, but DEGW discovered that most of it was actually vacant for more than half of a typical day. Not more space, but a better use of the existing was the recommendation.

Strategic briefing could be seen – wrongly – as an infallible method of determining the ideal size, layout, furnishing, servicing and overall look of a building, which magically materialises at the end of the process. DEGW's objectives in the strategic briefing process are not, however, to encourage architectural determinism: the idea that there is only one 'correct' solution. Rather, the aim is to lay down a strategic and overarching framework within which client, architect and other professionals may work to achieve optimum results. The end product should be a building which not only meets business objectives but, equally, is a good place to work in and live near. Above all, in DEGW's view, architectural design should be used strategically to act as a catalyst, stimulating the cultural changes that the practice has always promoted as central to business success in a changing world.

The User

'Users aren't bothered about their buildings; they just want to get on with their business' is a common response when people first consider the importance, or rather the lack of importance of the offices and other facilities they work in. From a narrow commercial perspective such comments are easy to understand and, in certain circumstances, the sentiment may even be justified. Successful companies under commercial pressure will certainly seek to drive down occupancy costs. To remain competitive, they cannot afford to spend a penny more on accommodation than their sharpest rivals. The problem with this way of thinking, however, is that buildings, by definition, become unimportant. They are swept off the corporate agenda and treated as commodities or, even worse, as consumables.

DEGW's focus on the user is driven by an understanding that organisations must control change at the point where people, process and place interact.

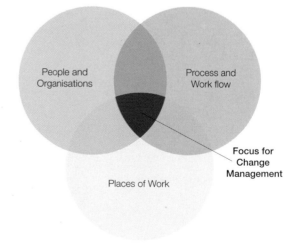

Clients may think buildings are unimportant, but then property developers and owners are equally convinced that their buildings' users are unimportant. Leave property to us, they say, we will take it off your hands. Clients never know what they want. Users always change their minds.

Self-actualization Needs
(self-development and realisation)

Esteem Needs
(self-esteem, recognition, status)

Social Needs
(sense of belonging, love)

Safety Needs
(security, protection)

Physiological Needs
(hunger, thirst)

Clients talk of short leases, ease of disposal, the need for change. In fact, they believe that clients demand a flexibility from business buildings that beggars belief.

But who is the client? Who is the user? There is an uncomfortably sharp contrast between the focused self-interest of the supply side of the property equation and the blurred indifference and alleged ignorance of the demand side – the clients, tenants and users. The chief executive of an organisation may hold one view and the property manager another, but both are supposed to represent the 'corporate user', that elusive entity that appears in so many traditional building briefs. The reality, of course, is that there are hundreds or even thousands of users in any corporate building. And part of what the developers say is true: they are always changing.

These multiple, shifting, changing, real-life users are quite different from the theoretical, unitary corporate user. They are much more important than it has been convenient to allow and are rapidly becoming more so. When questioned, it turns out that they are extremely sensitive to everything that supports or hinders their business life. They know that their productivity is affected by the location and suitability of the places where they work. However, they do not have a voice. The myth of the unitary corporate user has got in the way. This blockage explains the general poverty of the business environment – poverty demonstrated not just in the lack of attractive interior design, but also in the lack of creativity, stimulus and imagination that would help the workplace and its occupants to be more productive.

Many organisations, on both the demand and supply side of the equation, are searching for the key element that will support business best. Because of the disintegrated way in which most businesses are still organised, those who claim to have the answer tend to propose solu-

tions from their own discipline, from human resources, information technology and even, very occasionally, from design. Unfortunately, increasing productivity in modern businesses, especially if they are knowledge based, is an inherently complex problem and any credible solution must, inevitably, be systemic. In other words, the people who have to carry out the required work, the processes used to carry that work out and the place where the work is done must all be considered together as parts of a complete system. All three elements – people, process and place – are involved in change management and they have become a unifying thread in much contemporary management theory.

However, the emphasis changes. In the 1980s 'total quality management' (TQM) reigned supreme, stripping apart every business process in the search for greater efficiency. Since then 'business process re-engineering' (BPR) has taken over, adding organisational restructuring as an essential factor in speeding up the process of

69

Legal firm Baker & McKenzie reflects a traditional approach to office planning, with perimeter offices for the partners, and secretaries working without external aspect.

change. "It's big change, fast", says James Champy, a leading apostle of change management.

In the 1980s, information technology (IT) was thought to be the chief catalyst of change. The burgeoning power of IT enabled processes, impossible only a few years earlier, to be carried out in nanoseconds. Today, IT provides the platform to support the speed of change demanded by BPR, which is why IT, on its own, is no longer the key element in introducing change. IT is only part of a grander infrastructure of services. While technology enables change, it is the actual changes in working practices that bring real gains in productivity.

The conventional office is, of course, only part of an increasingly diverse range of environments where office work is carried out. Information technology enables office workers to work where they need – or, indeed, where they want. This runs counter to the old-fashioned management belief in 'presenteeism' that confuses physical presence with working, and assumes that

simply being at a desk is the same as being productive. Perhaps, given such deep-seated assumptions, it is hardly surprising that office workplaces have changed so little over the last century. Such managerial attitudes cannot survive for long, however. Nor can the office environment persist in its conventional forms.

DEGW has focused on office design for over 25 years. The growth of the service sector, the increasing importance of 'knowledge work' in the economy, the dematerialisation of office work and the consequent changes in working lives, timetables and locational patterns all mean that conventional design solutions are highly questionable. These changes also mean that the relations between users and clients, and the property and construction industries, must change radically. The increasing role of the facilities manager in the change process, the development of new techniques for involving the users in the design and management of their working environments,

The library at Baker & McKenzie. 'Knowledge work' is of increasing economic importance to all businesses.

and the need to adapt buildings quickly to meet emerging needs are all issues that need to be addressed now.

Since the late 1970s DEGW, more than any other design practice, has been an enthusiastic advocate of facilities management. In the last decade, the provision of facilities management services has been one of the few growth areas in the depressed British property and construction industries. In the United States, and internationally, facilities management has turned into a spectacularly successful movement. A new profession has been founded. The basis of this newly found professionalism has been the inevitable demand by business organisations for higher levels of competence in the management of real estate and other expensive physical resources in an increasingly turbulent business environment.

The management of change is an inherent goal of facilities managers, whose mission is to manage the accommodation assets of their company through time and in the most cost-effective way possible. Use, time and change are where

buildings and organisations touch. This makes the best facilities managers translators between the business world and design, facilitators between now and the future. Unfortunately, this is a difficult role that few facilities managers seem able or willing to perform adequately.

As a consequence, the facilities management movement as a whole, and on both sides of the Atlantic, has failed to accept what the management of change really means. One reason is particularly ironic: facilities managers have fallen into the same trap as conventional architects in that, in the office field at least, they have tended to over-emphasise the importance of tactical delivery at the expense of planning and achieving strategic business objectives.

Another reason for the failure of facilities managers to develop their full potential as the users' friend is the major changes in the pattern of business over the last decade, dramatically reshaped by the recession. Universal cost-cutting has led to widespread downsizing and outsourcing. All too often, facilities managers have seen

Change management theories since the 1950s and their level of influence. Unsurprisingly, workplace architects have struggled to stay abreast of trends.

Bradfield College, 1989-96. DEGW's expertise in organisational management is particularly relevant to modern educational needs.

their first priority to be cost-cutting rather than adding long-term value through the ever more inventive and ingenious use of office space. They have failed to anticipate strategic change and have been forced to become more and more reactive. Outsourcing of non-core activities, including facilities management itself, has further undermined the status of even the most professional facilities managers, forcing them away from the key end-users whose interests they should have been defending.

The development of a 'software' of facilities management, therefore, equivalent in importance and complementary to the design of the physical environment of the office, has been achieved only partially and imperfectly. DEGW has always been a strong protagonist in this process, although latterly in a much more impatient way, not least because the difference in quality of service between, say, hotel and facilities management has become increasingly apparent to our most innovative clients who are keen to experiment with new ways of working. Facilities managers might do well to look beyond the property and construction industry to real service providers, such as hotel managers who are trained to anticipate user demands and are rewarded for providing ever higher levels of service.

The Johnson Wax Building, 1938. Frank Lloyd Wright's cathedral of commerce relied on the subordination of users to its grand organisational and aesthetic plan.

The IBM offices at Cosham, 1971, were one of the first US-style open-plan workplaces in Britain. Architect Foster Associates introduced a new element of freedom, however, by making a feature of the exterior views.

Involving users in the design and management of their space is another way of saying that the design of offices and the provision of services are moving closer and closer. Empowering users to match their working environment to their work processes is essential if effective ways of using space and time are to be introduced. This proposition raises fundamental questions about how such environments should be provided.

The real users of a building are quite different from that notional and uncritical cipher, the 'corporate user'. Being so close and alive to the interface between environment and work, the real users are the first to experience any problems. Their attitude to environmental problems depends a great deal upon the processes used to achieve the physical result. DEGW believes that the more the real users are involved in the process of change, physical or organisational, the more likely the result is to be successful.

It is often said that people always resist change. If this were true, the challenge of inventing new environments for new ways of working would be huge. However, DEGW's research and design experience shows things are not as simple as that. Franklin Becker explains why: "Change prompts a reaction that is aptly compared to the grieving process. In many cases, people must experience the emotions of denial, anger and depression before they can accept the fact that major change has occurred.

"On the other hand, there are many types of change that people not only accept, but actively embrace; marriage, the birth of children, holidays, promotions, the mastery of new skills and so on. So the maxim 'people resist change' needs to be more specific.

Open-plan offices
for Grand Metro-
politan. A fast re-
sponse to change
must be balanc-
ed against loss
of individual iden-
tity or privacy.

"More accurately, people resist changes that threaten to undermine their sense of dignity and worth, devalue their personal and professional identity, strip away friendships and valued social contacts, or form obstacles to job and career advancement. People value changes that enhance personal and professional identity, social networks, skills and talents. The challenge is not so much that people resist change, but they resist change that they suspect has not been well designed and effectively managed."

Franklin Becker introduced the idea that a building's success has to be measured on at least three fronts: from the perspective of the architect, the owner and the user. Buildings are rarely successful on all three. Indeed, there are those who argue that success on all three is impossible. For DEGW, of course, all three priorities *must* be satisfied.

DEGW's offices for the University of Greenwich, 1996, reconciled the needs of the architect, owner and user.

There are all too many cases where companies have been convinced that changing the design of the workplace to match recent trends will automatically make a difference. During the 1970s, for example, many companies moved to open-plan offices. However, such offices have not enjoyed universal success because, as DEGW's

1978 open-plan study for IBM Europe showed, they can force users to prioritise between the goals of the corporation and their own individual inclinations – a dangerous option.

More openness, easier communications, more efficient use of space, a less costly fit-out, simpler space management and a faster response to change are some of the key corporate benefits from open planning, while increased noise levels, visual distraction, disagreements about comfort levels, lack of appropriate spaces for activities requiring concentration or privacy, as well as loss of individual or team identity, are all common concerns among employees. Conflicting performance criteria made evident by the open plan can, therefore, exaggerate the often inherent tensions between management and workers.

Companies that have attempted innovation in the workplace have sometimes done so hand-in-hand with more recent trends in change management. Stories abound about new office envi-

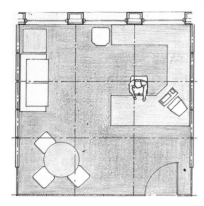

This study of an executive workstation explores how private work and interaction with others can be managed in open-plan or partitioned space.

ronments that have created more problems than they have solved. 'Hot desking', 'free address' workstations, 'hotelling' are not always working as well as had been hoped.

The explanation for these recurring problems lies in an imperfect understanding of the users and, in particular, of the detailed way in which they work and relate to one another. All too often corporate clients are blind to individual and operational differences. Deep down, simply for their own convenience, they want all users and operations to be the same. This is, of course, nonsense. The most successful examples of hot-desking or hotelling have occurred where the user population is out of the office for a high proportion of the working day or away from their base office for considerable periods of time. Not all businesses work in this way. Organisations that try to copy such solutions without taking such basic differences in working patterns into account are doomed to failure.

It is sometimes argued that if users are too heavily involved in specifying what is needed, they tend to spoil themselves rather than respond to real business needs. Similarly, it is often said that, if office accommodation is tailored too precisely to what users think they need today, flexibility to meet future requirements will be lost. And do users really know what they want? These important issues are at the heart of the current debate about new ways of working – and they are not new. For decades, the role of the user in the complex procurement processes that surround building provision has been fiercely contested.

DEGW's inclination has always been to include the users from the beginning and, indeed, in 1991 the practice established the Workplace Forum to accelerate this very process. The members of the Forum – for the most part senior property managers from major client organisations – meet several times a year, under DEGW's guid-

ance, to explore matters involving the design and management of new types of workspace. In this way, managers can rise above day-to-day pressures to compare problems, priorities and experiences and reach a common level of understanding. The Workplace Forum is, in effect, an ongoing, collective device which allows users to build up a shared body of knowledge about the impact of design on business performance – similar, in many ways, to DEGW's continuing series of one-off, multi-client studies.

As to the users' aspirations, their validity is not in question but their achievability has to be negotiated in the light of shared business needs. Business needs and personal priorities are not as distinct as they used to be. Rising expectations and unfolding user needs are becoming critically important to service providers. Many of DEGW's developments in briefing, such as pre- and post-occupancy survey methods, mock-ups, workshops and focus group techniques, have been designed to negotiate priorities and to explore solutions directly, face to face with users.

Arup Associates' office for PA Consultants compensates for the loss of individually owned workstations with a high-quality, work-anywhere environment.

Shell's new training centre at The Hague, Holland, rethinks what a learning organisation really requires by combining workplace with hotel.

Below: the lobby of the Shell training centre. New types of organisational users require new building types.

Workplace Envisioning, for example, which DEGW developed with Steelcase, is a computer-aided briefing process that allows large numbers of end-users to explore scenarios of change in an accelerated but quantitative and carefully structured way. Tom Peters draws attention to the 'WOW' factor, that element in the design which pleases users and clients alike by turning apparently trivial aspects of the office environment into nuggets of gold. Satisfying user expectations is, in itself, a powerful means of measuring the performance of the office environment.

Adapting the working environment to respond both to rising user expectations and to diminishing time horizons for decision-making is as much

for anything that might happen. Designing for adaptability forces everyone to join in predicting the future. And because it encourages shared responsibility in the decision-making process, it tends to lead to affordable solutions. How much adaptability is something that can be calculated after thinking through scenarios of change. To what extent and in what areas adaptability is needed are questions that help to inform realistic and sustainable solutions.

How, then, does adaptability overcome the problems of over-specific and 'timeless' design? Part of the answer lies in the modularity of design components, something that good space planners have always known. Modularity provides the ability to exchange one use for another. It works well with a menu of work settings generated by careful study of the users' needs, a key part of any intelligent design strategy. Adaptability also helps with the refurbishment of space. Remember that the majority of design work is to do with the re-use of existing buildings. Whether users are trying to fit technology into heritage buildings or new types of organisations into intelligent buildings, the principles that underpin the process are the same. Determine what the demand is before turning on the tap of supply – a simple message broken every day by every major corporation in the world.

Matching patterns of user demand with building supply is essential to any successful commercial property strategy.

a design issue as it is critical for management. Flexibility is a very convenient but expensive word that clients often use. For designers flexibility means redundancy, because it implies providing all the features you can possibly think of just in case they may eventually be required.

Adaptability is a much better – and much cheaper – term to use because it means including within the design the capacity to add features later: planning for change, rather than catering

76

DEGW's ideas about user needs have been influential on projects by other architects, not only in the private sector but in public life too. This is the civic centre for Chester-le-Street, by FaulknerBrowns.

Why is this? The problem is that corporate users without direct property experience are often completely unaware – until too late – of how dangerous real estate can be. The wrong buildings can kill. Buildings differ dramatically in their capacity to accommodate different kinds of uses. Facilities management procedures also vary wildly in their effectiveness. The measurement of these capacities and these differences is the key to relating building use to business performance.

Anticipating organisational demand for space is about more than just calculating the number of square metres required – not that easy, incidentally. Rather, it is about anticipating what quality of space will be required. In management terms, building quality means measuring the capacity of a building to accommodate changing patterns of use – such as the building's suitability for accepting both cellular and open-plan office space, for absorbing specialised areas such as a restaurant or conference facilities, for making people comfortable with the demands of new technology, and, above all, for broadcasting the right 'messages' to staff and to customers. Buildings are eloquent testimony of what management and users really value.

Matching demand and supply so that user needs are continually reconciled with building capacity is the basis of a successful real estate, property or facilities strategy. To achieve this in a time of change, DEGW has recognised that three requirements must be met: facilities management must achieve far higher levels of service and professionalism; users must be involved in space design and management to stimulate solutions that are far more innovative and cost-effective; and finally new design and managerial techniques are needed to make the working environment far more adaptable.

It is no accident that some of the most successful and innovative companies in the world – such as Andersen Worldwide, Sun Microsystems, Andersen Consulting and Boots the Chemists, all of whom DEGW has been lucky enough to work for – have already absorbed these lessons and are looking for ever more innovative ways of using office space to benefit, in the least time and in as many ways as possible, their rapidly expanding businesses and their increasingly involved users.

Consulting the User

"Universal solutions don't make sense, practically or financially", says DEGW's David Jenkin. That statement sums up a core element in the practice's philosophy – a commitment to understanding and then meeting the needs of the people who use a building. The same approach, in essence, underpins its work on a wide range of projects. And one project with

DEGW's addition to the Great Ormond Street Hospital had to relate to adjacent Georgian listed buildings.

which David Jenkin was closely involved was the new building at London's Hospital for Sick Children in Great Ormond Street, housing the Camelia Botnar Laboratories. At first sight, this scheme might seem far removed from the world of international business and large financial institutions. But the same basic organisational rules were applied: this was to be a building reflecting the needs of users.

The first approach from Great Ormond Street Hospital (GOSH) came in 1989. GOSH is a complex accretion of buildings of various dates, lacking clarity and convenience. Peter Hindley, the hospital's director of estates and capital planning, had the task of rationalising and modernising the GOSH campus. As part of this process, DEGW was asked to examine the hospital's pathology laboratories and to advise on the best approach to massive upgrading, whether this might be a refurbishment of the existing buildings – the laboratories were spread over several locations – or an entirely new block. Not surprisingly, the need for a single new building emerged quite quickly, and it was eventually built with the assistance of a major private donation from the Camelia Botnar Foundation.

The laboratories are a key part of GOSH's strategy for acute paediatric care and research into child health. The staff with whom DEGW worked up the brief for the new building are pathologists, researchers and technicians of international calibre. The site was a precious slice of land on the edge of the Bloomsbury campus, and it soon became clear that the new building would have to relate, both in bulk and overall appearance, to a context of early Georgian town houses. (Ideas of locating the building away from the main site

Early sketches show a straight-forward building, well tuned to the street. The main priority was to be a good neighbour.

The exterior of the new building defers to its historic neighbours without attempting pastiche.

were soon ruled out as the laboratories need to be close to the patients and operating theatres.) Even so, the new building was designed from the inside out, the product of an intensive dialogue with its future users.

Health service professionals, it emerged, tended to be rather cynical about architects. Too often, expensive new hospital buildings had proved technically deficient, anonymous, unfriendly and obsolescent even before they opened. The GOSH building had to turn that preconception on its head – and within a strictly controlled budget.

Shell and core, plus fit-out, was the route chosen to achieve this objective, so that the building could, if necessary, be stripped of its equipment and converted to another hospital use. Architecturally, it was designed around a deep, three-zone plan, with laboratories and offices to either edge, and the main services and vertical

circulation areas at the centre. As well as a number of small meeting rooms, this central zone incorporates lifts and stairs, lavatories and lockers, and coffee bars at every level that overlook a full-height atrium: places to relax and socialise and, perhaps, exchange professional news and ideas. Daylight and controlled air – precious commodities in central London – penetrate the heart of the building.

When a microbiologist was asked who had designed the laboratory in which he was working, he replied: "I did". There was truth in his comment. GOSH's senior management allowed DEGW unlimited access to end-users, placing confidence in the consultation process and accepting the need for the additional fee costs involved. Discussions were structured around an interview/questionnaire format developed for DEGW by Alexi Marmot and Joanna Eley. The aim was to establish what was needed – in terms of equipment,

This section of the GOSH building reflects DEGW's analysis of user needs. Laboratories and offices are arranged along either edge, while the central zone contains the main services and vertical circulation.

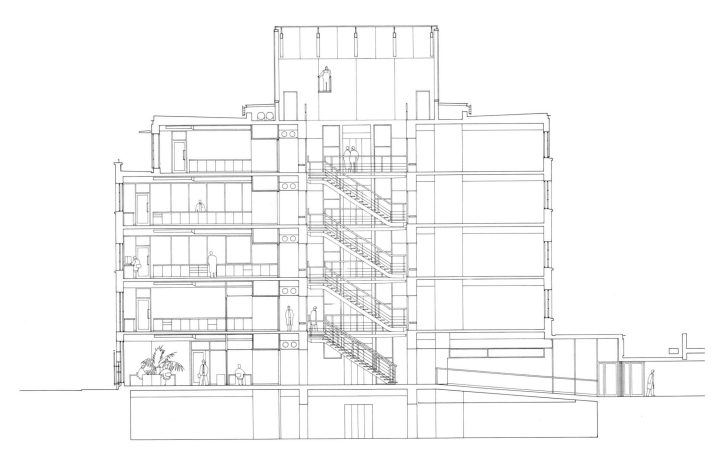

power provision, lighting and other technical requirements – and to explore people's personal preferences in terms of colours, finishes and other elements in the new interiors.

The process of consultation was designed first; then, out of that, came the building. "We had to learn the language of a different set of professionals", says Jenkin. "They proved to be willing and patient teachers, explaining in simple terms what their jobs entailed and how we could help to carry them out." The briefing process extended over nine months. However, communication with end users continued over the whole project – the building was completed in 1995 – although, inevitably, it was less intense during the two-year construction phase.

The architects "gained immeasurably" from the consultation process, says David Jenkin. "We felt that we had the confidence of the future users and we were determined to give them what they wanted." The GOSH project was highly innovative – a first for the NHS in terms of its use of the shell and core plus fit-out approach. The origins of this cost-conscious strategy lie in the field of commercial building. Yet the project has provided a hospital building which is both highly efficient and very popular with its users.

Bright colours are used throughout to enliven the internal areas.

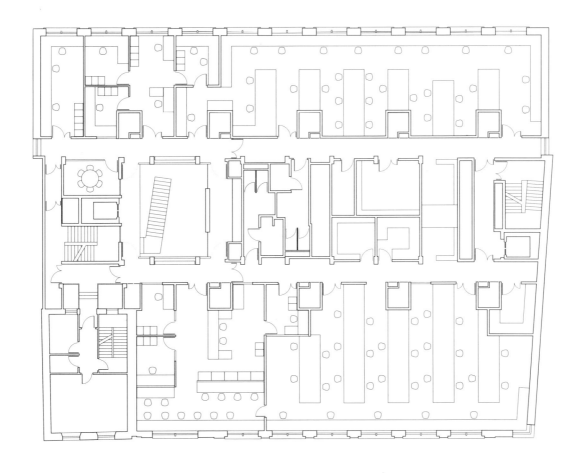

A typical laboratory floor showing clearly how laboratories and offices are sited to the edge. In this three-zone plan, the centre of the building is given over to staircases, lifts, lavatories, stores and meeting rooms, while a full-height atrium opens up the building to natural light.

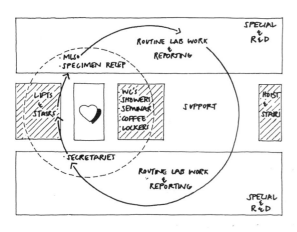

This diagram illustrates the way in which the building is used. The user facilities at the core of the building are central to the concept.

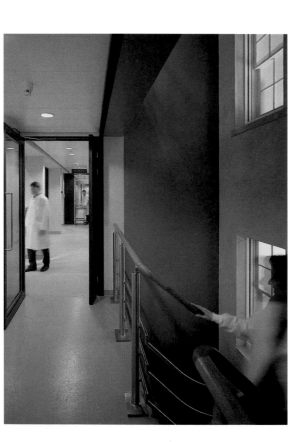

The architecture instils the building, which is basically little more than a highly specialised technical facility, with a sense of dynamism and movement.

Coffee bars overlooking the central atrium on each floor provide a place to relax. Users told DEGW exactly what they wanted from the building and the design responded to their needs.

The atrium is an uncompromisingly dramatic space, a point of focus at the heart of a densely built-up site, but one with a clear function in making the building open and accessible.

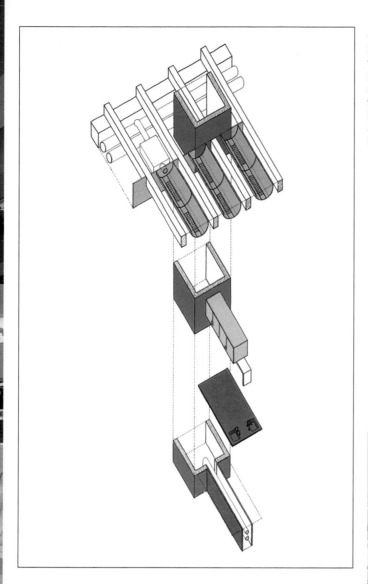

Careful planning has allowed DEGW to integrate the heavy servicing requirements of the laboratories into the structural fabric of the building.

The design of the fit-out and the choice of finishes reflect the importance of a perfectly clean environment.

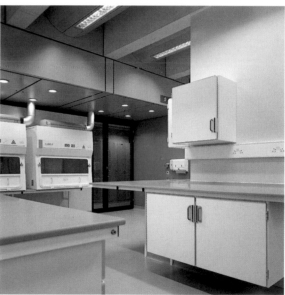

The layout of the laboratories as a contiguous space was designed in close consultation with the users to provide high-quality and easily adaptable working conditions.

Ceiling ducts reflect the heavy servicing requirements in a building closely linked to advanced research and treatment in child health.

In its previous headquarters *(top)*, Andersen Worldwide allocated most of the perimeter space to cellular offices for the partners. The new building **_(bottom)_ locates partners with the groups for which they are responsible, releasing the perimeter for use as meeting rooms and teamwork areas.**

The layout of the new offices is open and unenclosed, with plenty of space for informal meetings.

Before

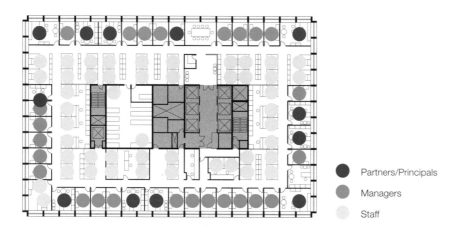

- ● Partners/Principals
- ● Managers
- ○ Staff

After

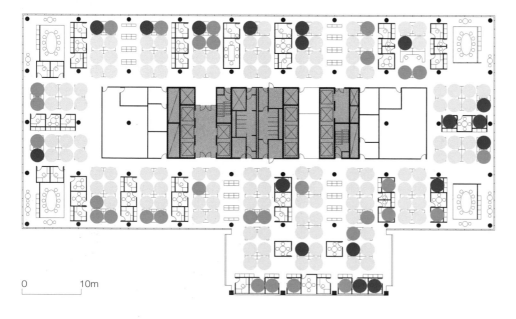

0   10m

The same concern for users' needs underlies DEGW's work with the Andersen organisation, the international consulting and accountancy business. Andersen Worldwide, the parent company responsible for supporting and servicing Andersen Consulting and accountants Arthur Andersen, has pioneered organisational change in the group. Despina Katsikakis, a director of DEGW, highlights the close personal contacts with top management as a foundation of a successful strategy for change. "It's a matter of real partnership, not the usual consultant/client relationship", she insists. "There has to be support, and a real drive to change, from the very top of the organisation."

At Andersen Worldwide, that support came from John Lewis, the company's chief financial officer and a passionate believer in involving and motivating his staff. Lewis spoke with approval of the ambience he experienced in a television studio – the air of activity, of people exchanging news and ideas. Business, he believed, had to cultivate something of the sense of urgency and immediacy so visible in media circles.

The underlying principles had been laid down in Andersen Worldwide's Global Real Estate Management System (GREMS), developed in the early 1990s – with DEGW

DEGW has designed the fit-out for a number of Andersen projects, including their main office in Brussels.

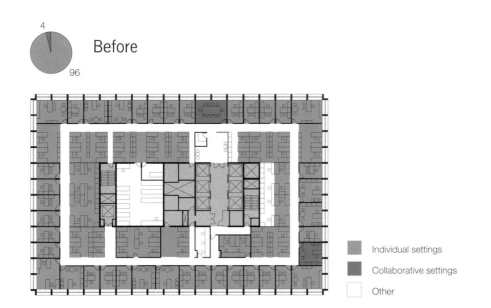

Before

4
96

After

30
70

Individual settings

Collaborative settings

Other

0   10m

as consultant – with the aim of providing financially and functionally effective office space for the Andersen organisation worldwide. John Lewis stresses that "it wasn't simply a matter of cutting costs". "The need to interact naturally and spontaneously with colleagues drove us to this project", he says, referring to Andersen Worldwide's 1996 relocation of its Chicago headquarters.

The physical implications of the move were straightforward: closing several existing offices in downtown Chicago and moving all 1100 staff into a refurbished Mies van der Rohe block in the Loop. The organisational implications were, however, radical and challenging. Interaction was the avowed aim. Yet half of the space in the existing offices was enclosed. Executives and senior managers valued their enclosed offices as a measure of their rank, but they were too often isolated in their enclosures, insulated from their staff and from the buzz of discussion and new ideas.

John Lewis saw established hierarchies as a formula for stagnation. A person's contribution to the company should be judged by his or her work, Lewis believed, not by titles or rank and certainly not by the size of their office. "It is a matter of what you do, rather than who you are", he declared.

Meeting rooms are generously provided, close to workspaces.

Cellular spaces in the new building are spread around the office floors, reflecting the new ways of working. Whereas most workplaces in the old building were 'owned', the proportion has now been drastically reduced to encourage greater mobility and teamwork.

Before

49 | 51

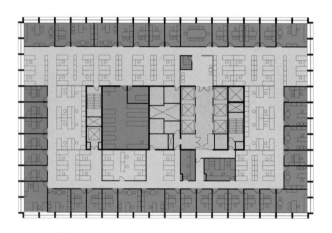

Open
Enclosed

26 | 74

After

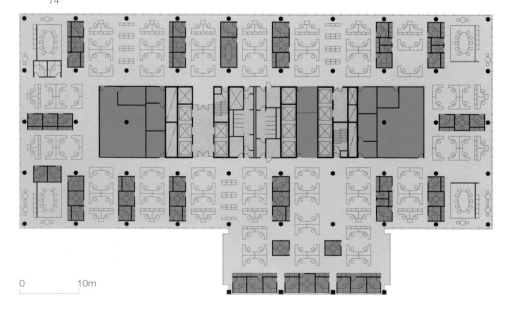

0   10m

Andersen Worldwide wanted a new culture of work, designed to get the best out of its staff and particularly to encourage team working. It was hoped that this approach would lead to a better use of space, with occupancy costs reduced and facilities used to optimum effect.

The initiative came from the top, but the company recognised the need to carry its staff with it – not least the executives whose privileges appeared to be under threat. Workplace performance studies revealed what did and did not work in the existing offices. A time utilisation study identified key statistics about the use of space over time – where people worked and for how long. Workshops were convened to garner opinions and ideas, and by the end of the process the DEGW team had met, face to face, around 80 per cent of the staff.

As at GOSH, people's working requirements and personal tastes were examined. The outcome of all this was encouraging: people wanted a more participatory management style. The usual office arrangements, it was felt, did not encourage communication or teamwork. While executives sat in their private offices, staff were provided with space that did not encourage concentrated work. Nor was the technical support adequate.

The main conference room of Andersen Consulting's main office in Brussels.

Before

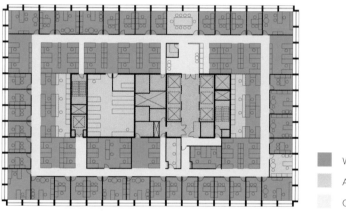

Workplace (owned)

Ancillary (shared)

Circulation

After

0   10m

As the results of the research process were carried forward into strategy sessions with user groups, and design concepts were drawn up, the vision of a new type of office emerged. It would offer settings for teamwork, with staff leaving their 'home bases' to join groups for specific tasks. The home bases would be arranged in neighbourhoods, themselves offering scope for individual and group activities within the team using the neighbourhood. It would be up to the team to configure the space to suit its own needs. Hierarchies of space were out. Executives and senior managers would work with their teams and long-prized corner offices would be given over to team activities.

As realised in the final fit-out, which was designed by Skidmore, Owings & Merrill, this vision has brought a space reduction of 30 per cent over the old buildings, although a staff reduction of 10 per cent took place as a result of the move. On a typical floor of the Mies building, density is 227 square feet per person – as opposed to 285 square feet in the old offices. Only a quarter of the floor area is enclosed. Collaborative workspace went up from a mere 4 per cent to 30 per cent.

There were some complaints, of course, and some executives

"Breaking down functional and vertical silos" was a bold move on Andersen's part and meant a far more collaborative approach to work.

As planned by DEGW and realised by SOM, the teams within the building are now able to interact with each other freely.

The Chicago project has inspired a mood of change throughout the Andersen organisation and the same ideas are now being applied, in different ways, to Andersen Consulting and Arthur Andersen offices worldwide. The strategy, Despina Katsikakis explains, is about space, innovation and performance, and its aim is to inform the company's approach to selecting buildings, to acquiring and fitting out the space within, and then servicing the whole. DEGW contends that it is possible to reduce costs of real estate, while increasing the satisfaction – and the pro-

resented the changes, but the solid consensus was pro-change, in favour of breaking down the 'functional and vertical silos' that John Lewis saw as an obstacle to progress in the company. Katsikakis insists: "Change management involves abandoning the old rules, which are all to do with imposing solutions on people. It means getting to know what people want."

The company sees the project as an outstanding success. It is popular with staff and appears to

be encouraging a climate of team effort, debate, experiment and innovation, which is all good for business. The new space, moreover, is designed to change and is already accommodating a steady shift to laptop computers and mobile phones. In retrospect, the old offices seem strikingly reactionary. But the new space is seen as part of a journey, rather than a destination – in achieving it, the company has come to a new recognition of the dynamics of change.

ductivity – of users. As Katsikakis points out, "the best modern workplaces engender a real sense of community, with the staff totally committed to their tasks".

90

Typologies

One way of dealing with the complexity of architecture is to classify buildings, and particularly their plans, into types – such as schools, churches and offices – each plan type in each culture being characterised by recurring and easily recognised physical features that often reflect specific values and particular purposes. The typological habit of classifying architects' plans has enriched and informed architectural history and architectural practice for centuries.

A typology, however, in architecture as in other fields, is merely a kind of shorthand. In fact, architectural typologies, because they tend to concentrate upon classifying architects' plans rather than the patterns of use that the plans are intended to accommodate, are particularly unstable, being constantly undermined by architects themselves as well as by the relation of architects to society – that is to say by the open-ended ways architects respond to the changing needs of the various individuals, organisations and institutions that use buildings.

Society sets the agenda and society moves on. It is up to architects to continue to invent new kinds of plan as well as to classify, for the convenience of fickle and volatile end-users, easily comprehensible ways of explaining what the huge variety of pre-existing plan-forms can offer in new situations. Perhaps it is only architectural historians who, constantly looking backwards and untroubled by clients, can enjoy the luxury of believing that architectural typologies are in any way fixed.

However, it is also true that DEGW has found the typological way of thinking about architecture particularly useful, from the very begin-

Durand's classification of building types proved very influential. This is the Hôtel de Ville at Poitiers, but near-identical examples can be found all over France.

nings of the practice until today. Why has the typological habit meant so much to a research-based and specialised design practice that has always been so closely associated with office design? What benefits has the classification of offices into types brought to DEGW's clients and to DEGW's architects and designers? In what ways have typologies helped to advance DEGW's design and research programmes? The first thing that must be said is that DEGW's use of typologies is neither conventional nor academic.

As an academic subject, modern architectural typologies can be traced back to the work of perhaps the leading architectural theorist of the early nineteenth century, Jean-Nicolas-Louis Durand. In 1800 Durand published *Recueil et Parallèle des Édifices en Tout Genre* in which he collected and grouped various international public buildings from several centuries according to his theory of modular proportions. This was followed by his major work, *Précis et Leçons d'Architecture*, a two-volume publication that led him to the conclusion that, if form followed function, an unforced aesthetic would result.

The essence of Durand's position was that all useful building types already existed and that each was defined by certain unvarying characteristics. Consequently, architectural 'design' never involved fundamental re-invention, but rather the intelligent application of informed planning skills to making the best use of a pre-existing type in a novel context. There is still a certain amount to be said for this approach – perhaps more than ever before in this age of CAD.

Durand, apart from being an architectural intellectual steeped in the enduring Classical tradition, was also an active instrument in the Napoleonic programme of modernising France, helping to train large numbers of architects quickly to erect the vast numbers of buildings – court-houses, schools, markets – needed to achieve the Emperor's social programme. No wonder, for practical as well as for ideological reasons, that Durand was so committed to articulating, transmitting and achieving a powerful, highly rational but deliberately limited architectural vocabulary. Moreover, there is yet another practical side to Durand's thinking – the proposition that the simplicity, order and repetition that come from a typological approach to architecture are in themselves an obvious strategy for delivering big architectural programmes and thus, paradoxically, for coping with rapid social change.

Le Corbusier's idea of the 'fundamental premise', of an appropriate and fixed set of architectural solutions reflecting specific activities, also formed an influential strand of thought at the Architectural Association in London during the 1950s. For a generation of AA students, Alan Colquhoun's reaffirmation that good design tends to modify types, rather than start from scratch, was particularly influential. To reject the lessons of typology was to be doomed to waste time and energy in continually re-inventing what already exists. In Colquhoun's argument, design as the mutation of type implies useful continuity whereas a rigorous return to first principles at every opportunity risks casting the architect more as an avant-garde practitioner – or even social engineer – than as a servant of society.

At the National Building Agency (NBA) in the mid-'60s, where Francis Duffy had his first work experience, the classification of plan-types for publicly funded housing was directed to the very pragmatic end of reducing variety in house plans to facilitate what was then called 'system building'. The published result of these variety reduction exercises, *Generic Plans*, was contem-

The generic 'off-
ice factory' or
'hive' plan evi-
dent in Frank
Lloyd Wright's
Larkin Building
of 1904 *(below)*
is preserved,
almost intact,

more than 70
years later in
Foster Associ-
ates' 1975 off-
ices for the in-
surance com-
pany Willis Fa-
ber & Dumas
(below right).

poraneous with the beginnings of the Cambridge
Land Use and Built Form Studies, evidence of a
somewhat differently motivated but contemporary
fascination among architects with the mathematical classification of architectural forms. The abiding memory of the NBA experience was how
easy it was, once the limited number of variables
that affected house plans within the constraints
of social housing were understood, to generate a
purely architectural typology.

However, there was something sterile and
unfulfilling about this work of classification. The

question of why variations should occur within a
purely architectural typology of house plans was
never really addressed. Nor was there any attempt
either to calibrate which plans worked best for
which domestic or economic or constructional
circumstances, or to explore what new mutations
in lifestyle might possibly occur that would justify the invention of new house types and the
rejection of outmoded models. It took another

A typological approach to analysing office space was explored in one of DEGW's most influential publications – *Planning Office Space*.

DEGW's scheme for British Gas in a converted warehouse relates the spatial concept of the 'hive' to the work process.

kind of experience to realise that architectural typologies could be related systematically to organisational typologies and that the resulting models that relate building and organisational types could be used dynamically to explore the architectural consequences of social change.

In the late 1960s Christopher Alexander provided the missing link by showing, in his book *Pattern Language*, that it was possible to use the typological approach to link architectural phenomena and sociological and, indeed, economic and psychological variables. Elemental propositions about what physical design ought to be like were systematically based on more or less testable evidence derived from empirical observation of how people behaved, that is, from the social sciences.

Whatever the subsequent fate of Christopher Alexander and his 'pattern language', this underlying lesson has been a tremendous influence on

DEGW. Giving equal weight to both physical and social data, treating both kinds of phenomena with equal respect and using one to test the other as rigorously as possible have become the three cardinal rules of both DEGW's research and DEGW's design.

Duffy's Princeton dissertation (1968-73) used such a bimodal and typological approach to bring equivalent architectural and social phenomena together in a systematic way in the field of office design. The objective, and to some extent the achievement, was to explain variations in office interior layout in terms of variations in organisational structure. To do that meant that it was necessary to model both sets of phenomena separately – physical and social – and then to measure quantitatively their relationship to one

DEGW redesigned its own London headquarters in 1997 as a laboratory for new ways of working, adopting a dynamic planning approach in which typologies play a key role.

another. What was, of course, novel about the model was that both architectural and social types were systematically identified, both were given equal importance, both were quantified, both were modelled independently and then both were brought together so that the changing relationship between the physical and the social could be systematically explored.

It is in this dynamic sense, rather than in the abstract working out of mathematical permutations or as a planning shorthand that allows shortcuts in the handling of constructional information, that DEGW continues to use the idea of typology.

The influence of the Princeton dissertation, completed significantly enough in the earliest days of the practice, upon DEGW's subsequent intellectual and design development has been fundamental. The structure of the practice, which brought the two streams of work in practical design and user consultancy together in one firm (not the easiest nor the most obvious thing to do), always attempting to give each equal weight, always trying to test design against user intentions, and never researching any social or organisational matter that doesn't have a design implication can be traced back to the principles that underpinned the Princeton dissertation.

Many of DEGW's research, consultancy and design methods – now, of course, immensely more sophisticated and elaborated – can be traced back to the same source. DEGW has held ever since that no typological system, physical or social, is ever complete or stable and that all such formulations are only useful if they are considered, in an environment of change, as inherently dynamic and open-ended.

Thirty years later, office buildings and office organisations are on the verge of bigger changes

than have ever occurred. Adding to the intrinsic challenges of the speculative office building and of the physical demands of widespread computerisation, comes that of the virtual office. Office work is being restructured. A new business geography is being invented in which offices are no longer located either in the suburban home or the city centre but at halfway destinations to save time, to minimise congestion and to improve the quality of life. Time as well as space is beginning to be used in the office in totally different ways.

New technologies in telecommunications and computers are transforming the workplace. At its new London offices, DEGW has introduced a more fluid approach to teamwork.

In the context of the dissolution of traditional conventions and accustomed boundaries the question again arises: what is the practical value of typologies today to DEGW and, more importantly, to DEGW's clients?

The answer is that DEGW sees the value of typologies as a vital part of a dynamic planning approach that is designed to champion the needs of end-users by exploring potential variations in architectural form that relate to their emerging needs, and by making the full gamut of new and old building forms accessible and comprehensible to clients so that they can understand how to exploit them for their own particular purposes.

The typological approach helps DEGW and DEGW's clients in a number of ways. For example, typologies provide the basis for collecting comparative data about buildings and organisations. This habit goes back a long way. The book *Planning Office Space* (Architectural Press) by Duffy, Cave and Worthington represented a comprehensive and very practical aid to architects and clients in the mid-1970s. Many of its insights are still relevant today, since it offered a detailed review of the general principles of office design along with specific guidance on decision-making at every stage.

it about the relation between society and office architecture that has allowed such differences to develop.

What can we learn from the comparison that will allow us to work out what is likely to happen next, when social and economic circumstances change yet again in both parts of the world? Very practical benefits have accrued. Typological thinking has facilitated the investigation of new

In modern offices, with their rapidly changing levels of occupancy and interaction, the coffee bar is often the most important focus for information exchange.

design challenges, for example, the problems associated with the distribution of cabling in office buildings after the explosion, in the early 1980s, of distributed intelligence. Mick Bedford and Paul Stansall's (1985) categorisation of cabling into primary, secondary and tertiary components – the major vertical distribution in the building core, the horizontal distribution on the office floors, and the local distribution at desk-

top height linking device to device – made it easy to identify that the worst design problems tend to occur at the junction between primary and secondary, or secondary and tertiary systems.

More recently, the same comparative typological approach, linking organisational and architectural features, has been the basis for the development, in a rapidly-changing business and technological context, of techniques for measuring the impact of architectural decisions upon organisational performance. The typological approach, once again, does not limit the search for novelty but, instead, facilitates the systematic search for new, more efficient and effective design solutions.

Yet still the economic forces at work today, in both speculative development and interior design, often militate against a comparable approach in building design. Standardisation, where it exists, is often of the wrong sort, being based not upon adaptable constants but on unthinking

Below: a 'cell' environment provides quiet and privacy for work requiring a high level of autonomy but low interaction.

cookie-cutter solutions. End-user satisfaction is frequently sidelined into addressing what best suits cost reduction while ignoring the legitimate demands of the real end-users. Certainly, the ideas long championed by Cedric Price for disposable short-term buildings, designed for the exact needs of the end-user, have not been taken up.

As we approach a new boom, only those speculative office buildings that are designed with the benefit of systematic organisational thinking will survive commercially. Only those corporate

users who have the imagination to link organisational development to design imagination are likely to procure buildings that will escape obsolescence.

In these circumstances DEGW has reapplied the underlying principles of typology in ways appropriate to today and, as far as possible, tomorrow. DEGW does so being in possession of an unrivalled body of analysis, data, research and practical experience gained individually and corporately over three decades, each of which has seen radical changes in office design.

Durand and Le Corbusier, although using the concept of architectural typology in very different ways, might even approve.

A 'club' environment is the perfect response to high levels of autonomy and interaction, but variable levels of occupancy. This is part of the new Scottish Enterprise office in Glasgow.

The New Office

DEGW has always insisted that the driving force of change in the office is the technology of information. Over the lifetime of the practice, the pace of technological change has accelerated rapidly. Coping with information technology (IT) has become the clearest imperative for business in the 1990s. Buildings have to be specified to cope with technological change if they are not to be overcome by premature obsolescence.

DEGW's ORBIT (Organisations, Buildings and IT) studies of the 1980s, produced in association with a series of client bodies,

DEGW's competition-winning masterplan for Stockley Park set the standard for the new business parks of the 1990s.

addressed these issues very directly. "DEGW has never been expert at IT", says Tony Thomson. "We worked with specialists, like Arup Communications. But we do make a point of stressing the demands of servicing buildings, envisaging the future needs of clients." The ORBIT studies were far from theoretical and had an immediate and lasting impact on the design of office buildings. Their findings made a strong impression, for example, on the briefs, developed in part by DEGW, for Broadgate and Stockley Park, benchmarks of new office design in Britain. ORBIT demonstrated that saving money on construction costs was a false economy for developers in the office market.

This was a lesson that struck home with a few enlightened developers – including Stuart Lipton, Godfrey Bradman and Geoffrey Wilson – who had no desire to create a new generation of second-rate buildings to succeed those of the 1960s. Instead, they actually wanted to enhance the public domain with high-quality buildings and civilised public spaces – as at Broadgate or Stockley Park – as part of a process of building in value. The latter development, in which DEGW has been closely involved from the start (the first building was completed in 1986), was driven by technological change.

The 'intelligent building' concept had been in circulation since the early 1980s and was initially understood as a matter of building information technology into offices. It seemed that the office building of the future would be a high-tech piece of machinery, packed with gadgetry to handle every aspect of the daily routine – from

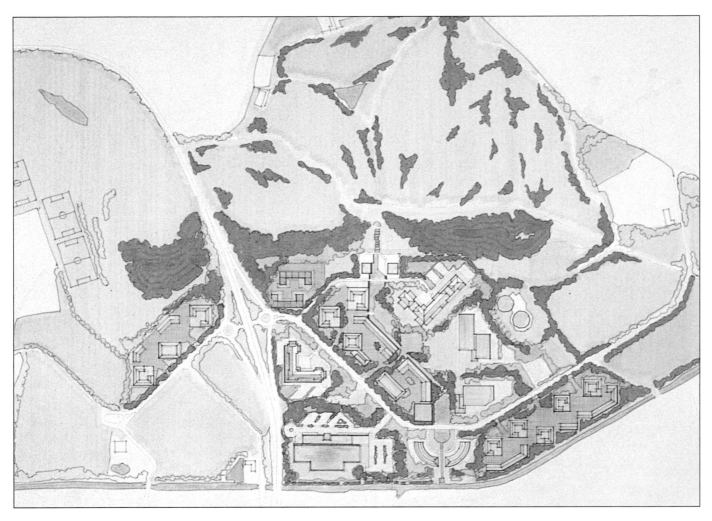

getting through the front door, to eating lunch and communicating with colleagues. According to Tony Thomson, however, "the intelligent building is a means to an end, not an end in itself. You need to think in terms of scaled-down technology. You can have a very effective workplace in a very simple building. Technology in itself does not make buildings 'intelligent'. You have to know how to use it".

The Intelligent Building in Europe study carried out jointly by DEGW and Teknibank in 1992 took the limelight away from the technology and directed it, typically, on to the user. It looked at the tasks that people carry out inside buildings. First and foremost, there is the core business of the organisation, be it accountancy, stockbroking or the management of a

car factory. The employees engaged in this business need to store, process, present and communicate information and knowledge. Second, there is the management of the building itself via human faculties and automated control systems. Finally, there is the management of space, which has to be used to maximum effectiveness in a way that accommodates change.

Out of these goals comes a series of key tasks – information management, managing change, minimising running costs, environmental control and human control over the environment – which can be used to frame the model of a building meeting an organisation's

needs. An intelligent building must respond to human needs at all levels. Again, the classic analysis of the elements of a building in terms of shell, services, scenery, and settings is used to good effect. Adaptability is vital. Some of the supposedly intelligent buildings of the recent past may have been over-specified, so that renewing the elements within them is not as simple as it should be – at worst, this can turn a building into a dinosaur. Stockley Park was to demonstrate the way forward.

The site of Stockley Park was a huge rubbish tip, a polluting eyesore which the local authority – the London Borough of Hillingdon – wanted to see removed. Initially, it was seen as ideal for a new

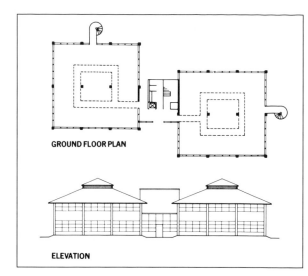

Stockley Park pioneered a new building type – neither factory, nor office.

GROUND FLOOR PLAN

ELEVATION

industrial estate, with an element of 'science park' – an American idea, then new to Britain – attached. At this time planning definitions relating to building uses remained relatively rigid, not least because the 'B1-use' classification, combining office, research and light manufacturing, was yet to be established. Indeed, the word 'industry' retained overtones of chimneys, noise and smoke. Stockley Park was a catalyst for the new business parks of the 1980s.

The site had been sold in 1983, with Stuart Lipton's Stockley plc as the new owner. DEGW had worked with Lipton on the Cutlers Gardens project, on the eastern edge of the City, when Lipton was a director at Greycoat. The practice had helped Greycoat to define the sort of tenants it wanted, even encouraging them to turn away those deemed 'unsuitable'. Lipton wanted to ensure lasting value and this included a mixture of the 'right' occupants.

Responding to concepts first developed by DEGW, Arup Associates designed a family of buildings tuned to the changing economy of the late twentieth century, offering open space that could be readily adapted to the needs of a wide variety of users.

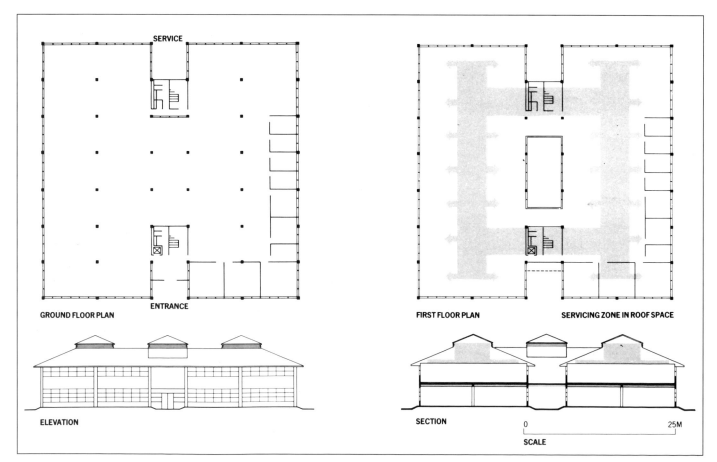

GROUND FLOOR PLAN   **SERVICE**   **ENTRANCE**

ELEVATION

FIRST FLOOR PLAN   **SERVICING ZONE IN ROOF SPACE**

SECTION

0   25M

SCALE

Architecturally, the finished buildings are relatively low, deferring to the green landscape that is such a prominent feature of the development.

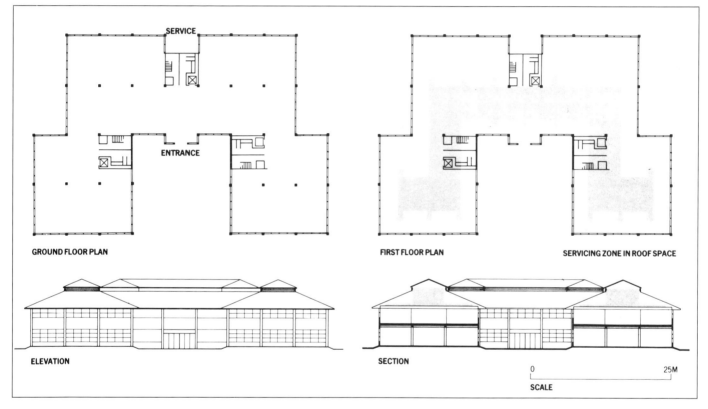

SERVICE

ENTRANCE

GROUND FLOOR PLAN

FIRST FLOOR PLAN

SERVICING ZONE IN ROOF SPACE

ELEVATION

SECTION

0   25M

SCALE

This approach prevailed at Stockley. The zoning of the site for industry was not a major problem, since Hillingdon planners saw that the meaning of that term had changed – Stockley, they ruled, was a place for "industry and research". In fact, it was often hard to define exactly the mix of uses in the various buildings.

The Stockley Park site was close to Heathrow and the M4 and within easy reach of the City and West End. From being a waste-land, it came to be seen as a valuable asset. High-quality buildings – including work by Foster and Partners, Ian Ritchie, Eric Parry, SOM and Troughton McAslan – and landscape were *de rigueur*. DEGW worked closely with Arup Associates, who also designed many of the buildings, on a master-plan and development brief.

User needs were a high priority, but who were the likely users? What sort of spaces and facilities would they want? DEGW developed a formula for site and buildings – adequate car parking, low-rise blocks, adaptable space geared to the needs of information technology, a sense of style and place, and flexible tenure arrangements that provided for mobility, growth and change. What emerged was really a new building type, unclassifiable in traditional terms.

The construction costs of the buildings, despite their highly distinctive character, were those of the industrial, rather than the office market, yet they retained plenty of scope for fit-outs to reflect the preferred styles of individual

Foster and Partners' 5 The Long-walk, offers a more forceful architectural image than some of the earlier buildings.

tenants. Research and development, engineering design, software development, and support and product development all happily co-existed. Moreover, the old ideas of the working day collapsed, with some staff working late into the night and at weekends and others spending very irregular parts of a highly mobile working week at the site. Since Stockley was a realm apart, well removed from residential streets, there was nobody to disturb.

Stockley Park, according to John Worthington, "exemplifies the shift from a service to a knowledge economy. It became a meeting place for exchanging information, where buildings and organisations seemed to 'fit together' naturally". The good fit was not, of course, a matter of chance but was the outcome of research and planning. Stockley is a major part of the DEGW story. Aspects of the project – its dependence on the private car, for example – are criticised a decade on, but it set the pace that others followed and, in its field, has never been surpassed. Research into building performance and user needs continued throughout the development process. Post-occupancy studies fed back into the later phases of growth and the close relations fostered between developer and

Though designed by a variety of architects, including Arup Associates, Eric Parry, Troughton McAslan as well as Foster and Partners, the individual buildings have been subordinated to the masterplan to create an overall effect of buildings in the landscape.

106

The quality of the landscaping at Stockley Park set the standard for all subsequent business parks.

DEGW's involvement with Stockley Park has continued up to the latest – and final – phase of development, with the preparation of briefing documents for the new buildings on The Square. Designed by Arup Associates, this building is occupied by CISCO.

tenants provided plenty of feedback. Stockley became a true partnership, to the benefit of everyone involved. In the late 1990s, it has lost none of its gloss.

"During the recession of the early 1990s", says Graham Parsey, "Stockley remained buoyant – because it was adaptable." Parsey began working on Stockley as soon as he joined DEGW in 1987. He cites Building 5, designed by

Foster and Partners, as a good example of Stockley's ability to provide for change. Parsey worked with the Foster team on the original specification for the building, which was designed to subdivide into three separate units if required. In the event, the whole block was let to BP, which chose to divide the whole building into cellular offices – an arrangement somewhat at odds with Foster's original concept. BP moved out in

1995. DEGW was subsequently responsible for the 're-conversion' of the building which, together with the adjacent Building 4 – by Arup Associates – was taken on by British Telecom.

British Telecom had evolved what it referred to as its Workstyle 2000 project as a response to pressing business priorities which made a clear case for a mobile

108

The entrance to the CISCO building. A cruciform plan-form for the offices within maximises the penetration of daylight and views out.

workforce operating in a new way. Part of the solution was relocation from city centres to city fringes – like Stockley Park – but the core of the project was about accommodating people, not machines, and giving them the right places to work. BT wanted office space in a 'club' style, suitable for teamwork, so that the cellular plan was completely inappropriate. DEGW's redesign was, therefore, calculated to encourage interaction. Completed to a fast-track programme and to a strict budget, it has given BT exactly the space it needs and one highly appropriate for a fast-changing organisation.

The BT project was achieved so efficiently because the building had been configured for change. As John Worthington insists, "a good building should have common sense". Basic issues of layout, servicing, and adaptability matter more than technological hardware. DEGW's involvement with Stockley Park has continued into the latest – and final – phase of the development around The Square. There, the new generation of buildings reflects a change in emphasis, with the abandonment of any pretence at a 'warehouse' look, for instance, and the introduction of opening windows. But the basic principles of the mid-'80s still hold good.

Today, the workplace may be becoming more sophisticated as

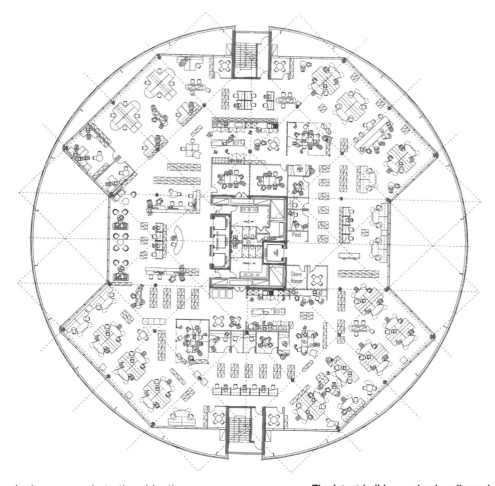

design responds to the objective facts of a world economy and an information age, and addresses the demands of the users for better working conditions and for direct involvement in planning their own environment. But the proper response, as DEGW has stressed from the beginning, is not an obsession with technology but with its proper use: serving people.

The latest buildings by Arup Associates represent a distinct evolution of the established form which responds to the latest thinking in space planning. More importantly, their simple, all-enveloping outer glass walls create a buffer zone round the offices themselves, allowing a high degree of natural ventilation and user choice.

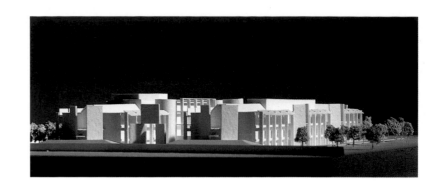

The planning of the building and its setting, with courtyards, planting and the use of pools, is designed to mitigate the region's hot climate. The plan is highly adaptable and can accommodate open-plan or cellular offices, as well as meeting rooms and other shared spaces.

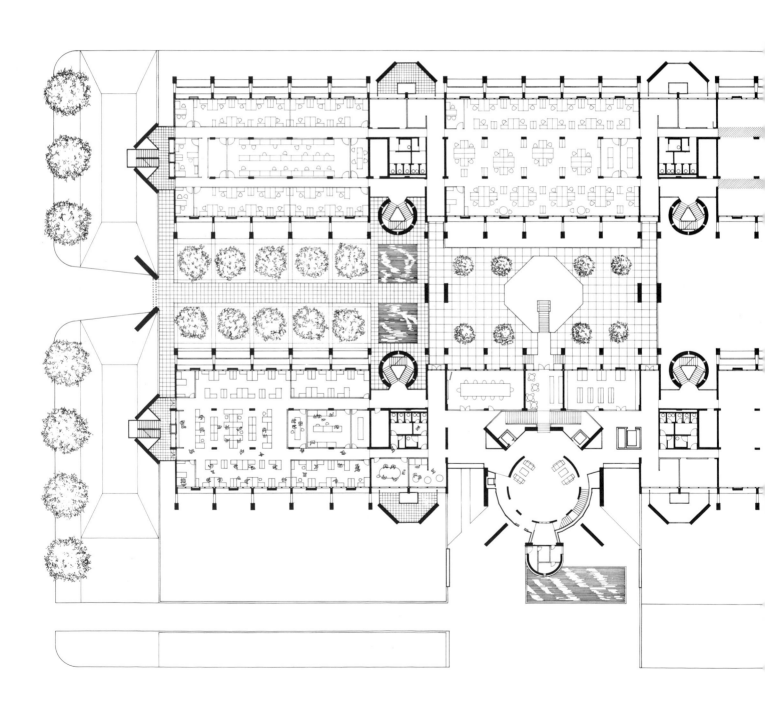

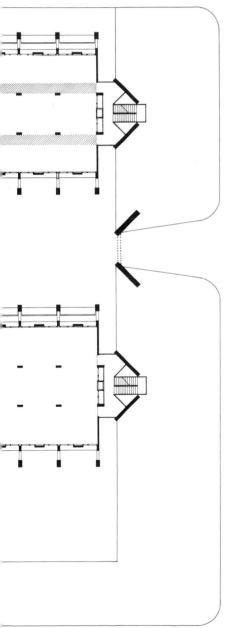

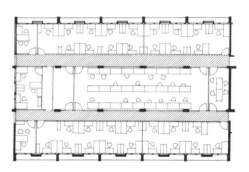

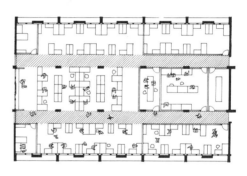

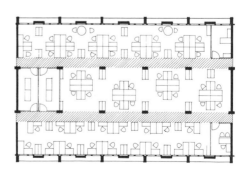

extreme dissimilarities in environmental conditions between the two locations.

Designed for a temperate climate, the Stockley Park buildings are lightweight in construction, with large expanses of clear glazing and full air-conditioning. The Bari building, on the other hand, is constructed in massive concrete, exposed inside and out, and lined with a protective barrier of heavy sun breakers. These protect the interior from the dangers of direct sunlight, while the thick concrete walls protect the whole building from the searing conditions usually encountered in that region of Italy during the summer months. Even so, this is a mixed mode building which is only partially air-conditioned – an extraordinary achievement for a High-Tech building in such a climate, and evidence of DEGW's insistence on the systematic coordination of plan, structure and interior climate.

Curiously, given DEGW's overt and programmatic rationality, the section, plan and external form of the Olivetti building, in particular the strong emphasis given the service cores, recall a more complex architectural tradition and demonstrate an abiding respect for the pervasive influence of Team X and the work of Louis Kahn, Aldo van Eyck, Herman Hertzberger and the Smithsons.

The architecture of the completed building is within a regional tradition, using solid and void to strong effect.

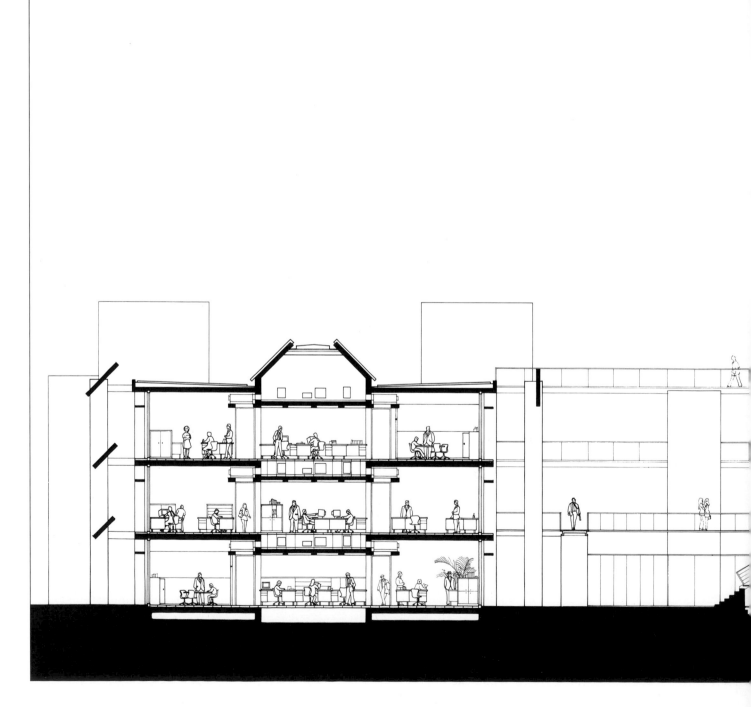

The central court at Olivetti is an attractive feature, but has a sound practical rationale in encouraging the flow of fresh air through the adjacent buildings.

A cross-section through the final design, showing the entrance pavilion with its triple-height interior on the right, separated from a typical office wing *(left)* by a generous open-air courtyard. The plantrooms and main service runs are kept within the cool basement.

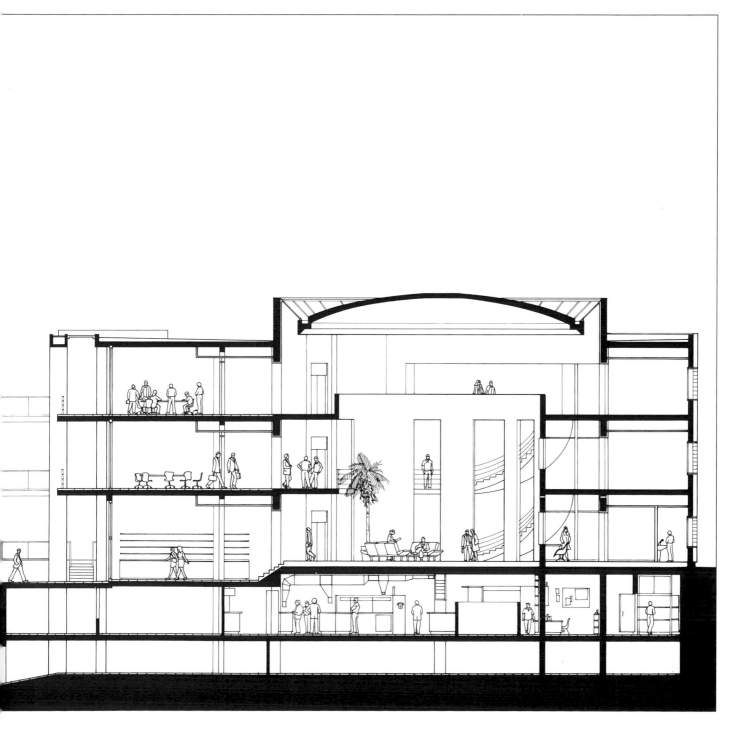

Light and Air

One reading of the evolution of the office building is the story of light and air.

Growing environmental awareness has resulted in a crop of British office buildings with a particular architectural vocabulary of ventilation chimneys, undulating exposed concrete soffits, light shelves and glazed atria that demonstrates a marked preference for natural ventilation – or, at least, for mixed-mode environments – rather than for totally sealed and air-conditioned buildings. This vocabulary is presented in a variety of styles, from Hopkins' Inland Revenue retro-tech in Nottingham to Short Ford's retro-gothic labor-

Michael Hopkins made explicit links between environmental control and building form in his Inland Revenue Building, Nottingham.

atories at Leicester's De Montfort University. Office building form in these recent examples is so closely related to interior climate and comfort that a worry lingers that such highly engineered structures and deeply integrated services may be over-prescribing function and limiting organisational adaptability.

In workplace design architectural forms derived from environmental systems have a distinguished pedigree. Ever since Reyner Banham's *Architecture of the Well-Tempered Environment*

116

(1969), the Larkin Building by Frank Lloyd Wright has been cited as a forerunner of integrated low-energy design. But it is important to put this seminal building in context. Larkin was designed for a single unchanging use as a clerical 'factory', a mail-order clearing house. The building's floor-plates, generally only about 20 feet deep, could have been cellularised only with the greatest difficulty.

Wright's example provided the intellectual impetus for later innovations: Louis Kahn's declaration that he "hated" ducts led to the San Giminiano-like towers of the ill-functioning

The Queen's Building at De Montfort University, Leicester: Short Ford's retro-gothic vocabulary for a naturally ventilated building.

Richards Medical Research Building in Philadelphia (1957-61). Larkin, for architects, stands alongside another landmark office building, Herman Hertzberger's Centraal Beheer in Apeldoorn (1973), a very literal transcription of Levi-Strauss's then popular preoccupation with structuralism into architectural form. The geometrical form of individual small 'trays' for group work within a plenum determines space utilisation – with never more than 12 people per tray. The highly individualised form of the building is literal both in insisting on small group working and in the liberal ethos it expresses.

Larkin advanced a more collective ethos in overt moral as well as spatial messages to the workforce. That working there was meant to be good for one is made very clear by the embossed texts looming over the Larkin workers: 'Whatsoever ye would that others should do unto you, do ye even so unto them'.

In the diametrically opposite architectural camp, Venturi, Scott Brown have long argued the case for generic 'loft' buildings in which the architect's role is essentially iconographic. At their

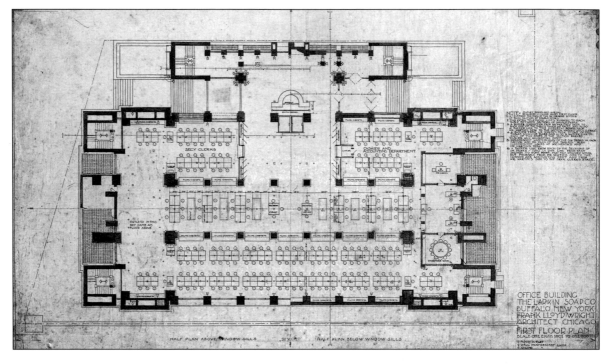

The Larkin Building's first floor plan expresses the needs of management supervision as clearly as the corporate slogans embossed on the interior walls.

laboratories for the Universities of Pennsylvania and Princeton (1985-88), Venturi, Scott Brown & Associates designed only the external skin of the building and such elements of the internal scenery as the entrance halls and common rooms. The highly adaptable workplace interiors were actually designed by the laboratory experts, Payette Associates. DEGW's laboratory building at Great Ormond Street Hospital (GOSH) is not dissimilar. Its two very different elevations are also iconographic, one conservation 'warehouse', the other utility.

Such a deconstructed approach seems to fit perfectly with DEGW's life-cycle based analysis of workplace buildings into 'shell, structure, services, scenery and settings' – but there is one big difference. Venturi, Scott Brown's loft buildings are invariably sealed, and fully and conventionally air-conditioned. Even more significantly, Venturi's

'generic' buildings depend on service cores buried deep in the plan, without formal or structural expression, surrounded by a perimeter race-track of circulation and workspace. The Venturi/Payette model lacks an organisational heart. No hollowing out of the interior is permitted. These 'decorated sheds' are simply deadpan, pragmatic, campus backdrop. If anything, they are under-engineered with no attempt to exploit the floorplate or the fabric as part of the servicing system.

In contrast, at GOSH, DEGW has inserted a highly visible, top-lit, vertical well of circulation and social areas to fit within the compressed confines of a tightly-grained, jealously conserved, central city site. DEGW argues that decorated sheds with their race-track spaces and amorphous service cores are not enough, and yet Venturi's

Hertzberger's
modular floor
plan at Centraal
Beheer, with its
small 'trays' of
12 people for
group working,
reflects a liberal
ethos untypical
of the period.

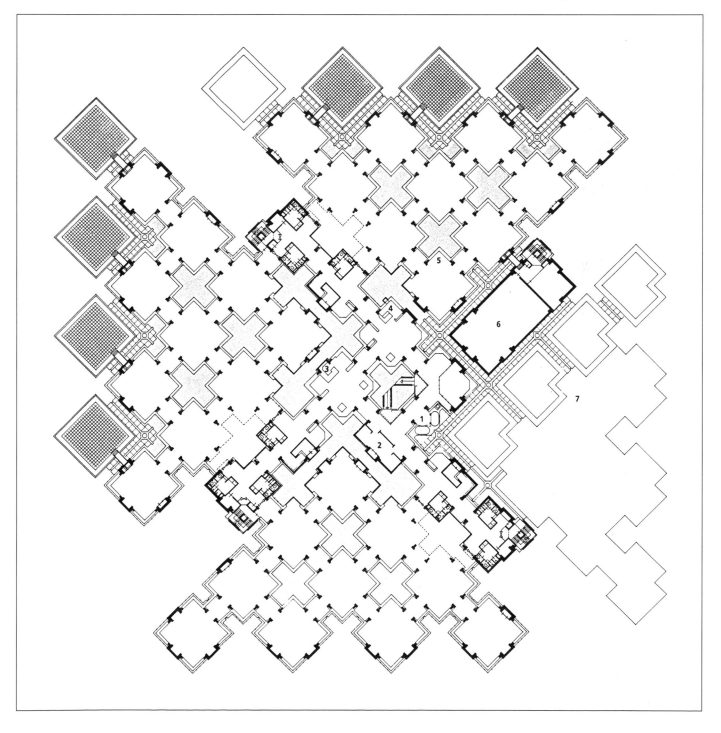

Foster Associates' new headquarters for the Hongkong Bank, 1986, owes a typological debt to Larkin but its larger scale is infused with light and air.

undemanding buildings are hugely popular with their American users.

The argument between Venturi, Scott Brown's programmatically generic buildings and the polemically form-driven, low-energy, highly-engineered designs of Alan Short or Michael Hopkins is complex. It may be that a simple, under-engineered, off-the-peg servicing solution is better future proofing than a highly specific one. The Venturi, Scott Brown laboratories may well be a better bet for 50 years of useful life than Hopkins' Inland Revenue building. The question is: how would we ever know? The answer has to be by the test of long-term utility.

Venturi would doubtless argue that the iconography of DEGW's Saudi Arabian office building for Apicorp (now under construction), with its highly articulated service cores, follows a form-

driven aesthetic, continuing what he has called, "Modern architecture's hang-up with grain silos". Like many buildings, from Frank Lloyd Wright's Larkin to Louis Kahn's Richards Laboratories, Apicorp is, by Venturi's standards, over-engineered and, therefore, over-designed. However, such a 'cultural' critique would side-step something that interests DEGW a great deal: the triangular relationship between architectural form, the use of space and the provision of light and air.

Venturi, Scott Brown tend to discount where cores are located, to ignore how the air supply is distributed around a building, and to underestimate the ways in which daylight is allowed to penetrate the skin. DEGW believes that these factors are critically important in determining the long-term effectiveness and efficiency of build-

An early design model of DEGW's office extension for Boots the Chemists. The original 1968 SOM-designed building is in the foreground.

ings – features that vary greatly between shallow- and deep-plan buildings and between buildings with cores on or off the floorplate. DEGW's own recent explorations of these issues swing between the generic and the specific, between constructional rationality and long-term utility.

The much admired Larkin building has never been copied. Nor, incidentally, was Hertzberger's Centraal Beheer. Larkin's floorplates, although well daylit, were too small to provide the standard commercial option of a double-loaded corridor, or an inner and outer office layout – unlike Adler and Sullivan's more conventional Guaranty Building in Buffalo (1895-96). Such options were not possible in a sealed building with supply air provided through hollow downstands to the atrium balustrades.

Yet, typologically, the Larkin Building is not very different – other than in scale – from such key office buildings of the 1980s as Richard

Rogers' Lloyd's of London or Norman Foster's Hongkong Bank in Hong Kong, both opened in 1986. The big difference is that the much larger and deeper floorplates of these modern examples are liberated by the combination of service cores at the perimeter and supply air evenly distributed and withdrawn through the access floor or ceiling voids. These supply and return air 'sandwiches' make possible an architectural language of translucence: buildings with balustrades which are invariably glazed and upstand free, fenestration which is full-height and frameless, and cathedral-like atria full of light and air. Even the structural frame is detached from the diaphanous skin. Each part of the constructional kit of shell, structure, services, scenery and settings has its own visual expression, and each is matched by a clearly delineated process of procurement and delivery.

The effect of this design approach on the organisations that use these buildings is power-

At the Richard Rogers Partnership's Lloyd's Building, 1986, perimeter service cores were employed to create an architectural language of transparency and communication.

121

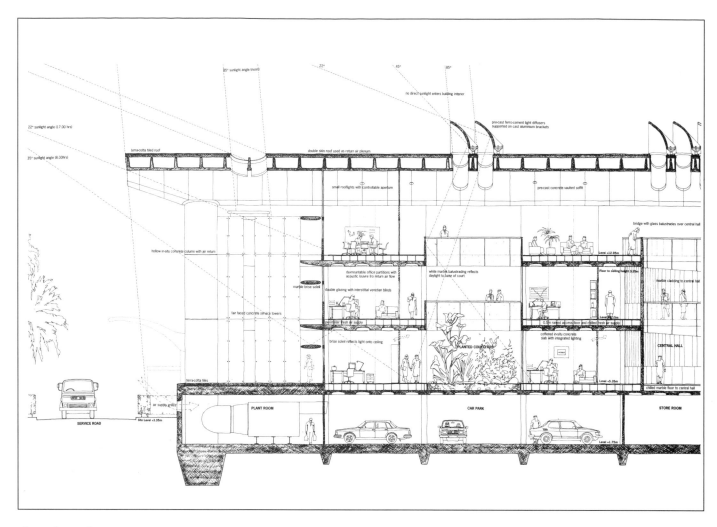

An early section through DEGW's Apicorp building reveals the three-way relationship between architectural form, the use of space, and light and air.

fully but unintentionally prescriptive. Hertzberger's emphasis on the group at Centraal Beheer is achieved at the expense of the corporate whole; Wright's Taylorist project at Larkin depended on paternalist bureaucracy; Venturi, Scott Brown's loft laboratories turn out to be aggregations of so many 'rented' rooms behind their iconographic, if self-consciously 'ordinary', punched-hole window facades; and the Hongkong Bank's inspiringly clear, loft-like, futuristic floorplates, surrounding a cathedral of light, paradoxically house nothing more than old-fashioned clerical work.

But, in DEGW's terms, all these examples are limited because they lack the potential to be adapted over time to accommodate the full spectrum of rapidly changing work patterns. Centraal Beheer is essentially a series of dens; Venturi, Scott Brown's lofts are cells or dens; Wright's and Foster's forms are inherently hives. And yet we know that most clients need buildings that can provide all four kinds of workplace in different proportions at any one time.

This is exactly the programmatic challenge that DEGW set itself when invited, in 1995 and 1996 respectively, to design the new headquarters for Apicorp and Boots the Chemists. It was

possible to draw on an immense collective experience of the briefing, building appraisal, planning and fitting out of hundreds of buildings by other architects, to anticipate the accommodation of as full a range of user options as possible. It was equally impossible for DEGW, given its history and design inclinations, to hold back from addressing fundamental environmental issues and from using architecture as a powerful means of creating places.

The clarity of the Rogers/Foster model and the liberating power of the 'air sandwich' are highly attractive. However, DEGW had discovered in refurbishment projects that, although a raised floor plenum might be all that could be achieved, a displacement ventilation regime would provide as much spatial liberation as air-conditioning could provide, but with nothing like the same demand for energy.

The first example was in the comprehensive refurbishment of a standard '60s developer's slab building for the Department of Trade and Industry (DTI) in 1995/96. This most ordinary and unprepossessing of buildings was stripped back to the frame and retrofitted with an environmental control system which permits a greater fluidity of movement and change than the original building was ever designed for. Power and telecommunications are made available to any part of the building beneath a raised floor which also acts as a supply plenum for fresh air. Combined with shallow chilled ceiling panels, rather than fan-coils and return-air ducts in a deep suspended ceiling, this has allowed the building – which could not sustain both a raised floor and a suspended ceiling – to be brought up to the highest commercial standards. The test is whether this one-off solution can be made to have wider application.

The DTI has long thin floorplates, ideal for cells and dens but not particularly suited to hive or club working – ideal, therefore, for a government department which has downsized and made the shift from a cellular to an open-plan mode of working. It may not be so well suited, however, to more radical space-planning solutions or for creating a more interactive workplace.

Refurbishing buildings like the DTI teaches many salutary lessons about stretching use potential. There is an abundance of such robust buildings – and not just in the UK. They often have greater plot ratios than would be permitted in a replacement. They can be easily upgraded or converted into hotels or residences, or used for education or for any mixture of these uses. And they can be radically restyled, as was the DTI, with the addition of a simple, sparkling new entrance pavilion.

Another kind of unprepossessing and ubiquitous building type is the large 'shed'. No longer suitable for manufacturing and storage alone, these simple 'warehouses' have accepted ever more diverse uses as, one after another, the museum, the shopping centre, the cinema, and the sports

hall have all been subsumed. Such buildings can also provide good office space, as DEGW discovered when refurbishing a high-bay warehouse for British Gas. This building, while not good for cellularisation, proved to be ideal for hive working and for a series of dens, sheltering under the collective roof.

If the framed slab blocks and simple sheds of the 1960s are overcoming their own conventional architectural typologies, surely invention will become more difficult for the designers of new office buildings. For DEGW, known best

Completed in 1896, Adler and Sullivan's Guaranty Building in Buffalo provided a blueprint for the modern office which was to last for the next 100 years.

The enclosed interior for British Gas *(right)* contrasts with the openness of the Arup Associates workplace for Wiggins Teape *(below)*, a key project in terms of exploring the benefits of internal and external landscaping.

in the 1970s and '80s for fitting out other architects' buildings or regenerating warehouses and frame buildings, this is a particular challenge. However, these adaptive experiences and the parallel refinement of DEGW's own thinking about new-build floorplates, together with the application of an ever expanding body of research, have stimulated the design of DEGW's most recent workplace buildings.

One simple view of this new body of work is that it is just another step in the gradual evolution of workplace design. These new buildings have been designed to combine the best aspects of the frame, the shed and the deep floorplate, continuing a line of development in office design

that began with our work on the Martin Centre in the 1970s. With its mixture of pavilions and courts, this building entered the world of office design with a seminal paper by Duffy, Hawkes and MacCormac in the *RIBA Journal* in 1976. Other important precedents include Colin St John Wilson's unbuilt headquarters for Lucas and a sequence of Arup Associates buildings in the late 1970s and early '80s, most notably for the Central Electricity Generating Board and Wiggins Teape.

The emerging typology in DEGW's current new office designs is that of sheds and courts, large enclosures within which several decks or floorplates of various depths surround daylit internal courtyards that act as lungs for displacement ventilation. Instead of extracting air through suspended ceilings at every floor level, a single large-span roof is incorporated into the design to serve as a low-velocity, return-air plenum over a low-rise but deep-plan building.

A more complex reading is that DEGW's clients are now increasingly demanding much more adaptive buildings, 'future-proofed' to anticipate changing work patterns, from cellularisation to open plan, practically everywhere. But there is

A detail section
through DEGW's
refurbishment of
the DTI offices in
London: a lesson
in how robust
buildings, seem-

ingly at the end
of their life, can
be reinvented
through the ef-
fective use of
light and air.

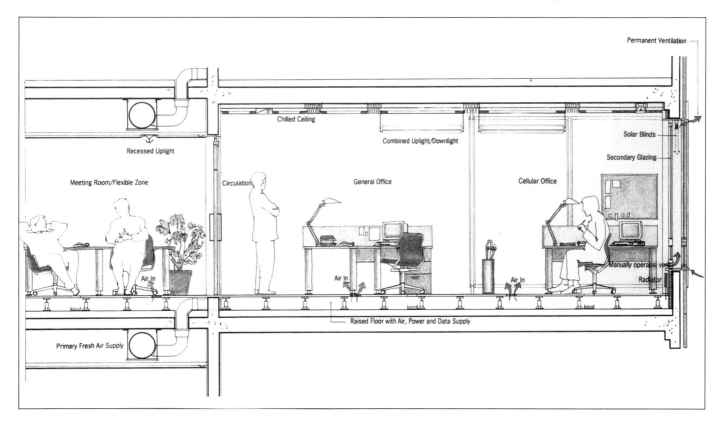

Permanent Ventilation

Chilled Ceiling

Combined Uplight/Downlight

Recessed Uplight

Solar Blinds

Secondary Glazing

Meeting Room/Flexible Zone

Circulation

General Office

Cellular Office

Air In

Air In

Air In

Manually operable vent

Radiator

Raised Floor with Air, Power and Data Supply

Primary Fresh Air Supply

more to it than this. These new plan-forms, consisting of an array of small courts ranged around a larger central atrium, are an attempt to make workplaces which can accommodate changing needs. They are being designed to combine, at any time in any one building, the extreme emphasis on the group found in Hertzberger's buildings as well as Wright's collective vision of a greater whole, with the clarity of Foster's big clean floorplates and Venturi, Scott Brown's knock-about, loose-fit lofts.

Our analysis is that a range of unequally-sized floorplates in one building can adapt to cell, den, club or hive working without prescribing the size of neighbourhood groups. They can also provide workspaces that are not only fit-out friendly but are also equipped with central shared spaces which celebrate the collective spirit of the organisation. Boots the Chemists' new headquarters in England's typically temperate East Midlands is designed in exactly this way, as is Apicorp in the inhospitable climate of Saudi Arabia.

The Right Environment

The extension to Boots the Chemists' headquarters in Nottingham is composed of large, unequally-sized floorplates, interspersed with an array of central and perimeter atria. These are necessary for the flow of return air, but they also reinforce the user-oriented concept of the 'office village' as a series of neighbourhoods linked by streets and sheltering under a big roof. The design is in stark contrast to the floorplate of the adjacent D90 building, designed in 1968 by Skidmore, Owings & Merrill, with its single, dominating, yet inhospitable open-air courtyard.

structure than Apicorp, with a simple long-span trussed roof that doubles as the return-air duct, cores that are compressed at the ends of the building, and an array of small atria pushed to the perimeter and lit from the edge as well as above. This design is the result both of the refinement of principles and of budgetary constraint. But though Boots is almost twice the size and half the cost of Apicorp, it is no less 'intelligent' a building.

In Apicorp, which was the earlier design, the more elaborate double-skin roof also forms the

DEGW's new building for Boots had to relate to the listed D90 block, regarded as a masterpiece of 1960s design.

Boots is closer to the new generic model of energy-efficient, 'loose-fit' buildings, while the smaller and earlier design for Apicorp is a more integrated design. The design principles applied to Boots have resulted in a less expressive

building's return-air plenum. Air is pushed through the building by displacement ventilation from the raised access floor plenums, rises to roof level, enters the roof structure, then is drawn back via vertical 'ducts' to the plantrooms in the plinth for heat recovery and re-

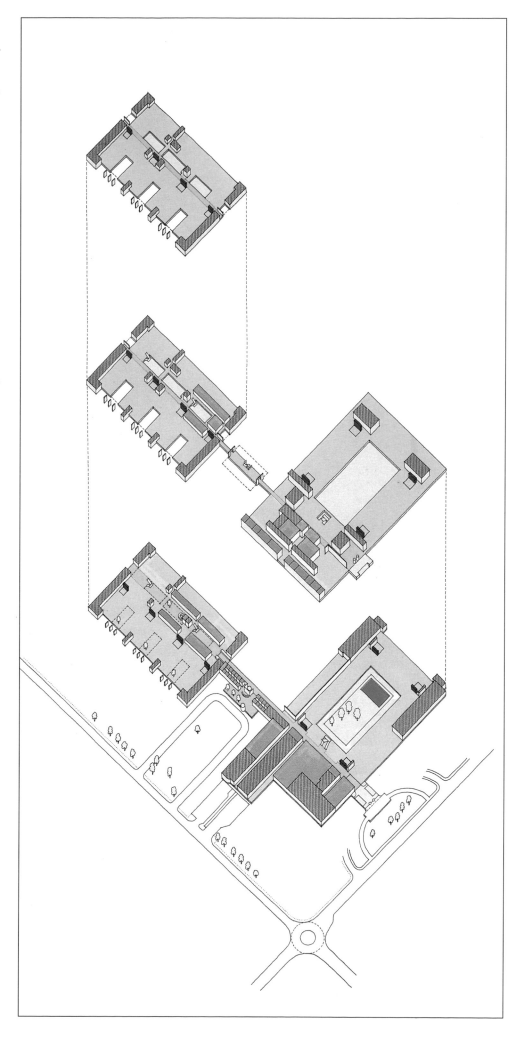

DEGW's new three-storey extension acknowledges the rational plan of the original building, while retaining its own identity.

circulation. These ducts – and this is the daring part – are also the cores of the hollow structural columns that support the floating roof. The Apicorp building is a prestigious headquarters building and its barrel-vaulted roof is its architecture. Underneath the curving canopy, the 'box' of office space is essentially a shell-and-core floorplate building, although the outboard cores are expressed as free-standing 'silos'.

Apicorp's environmental engineering strategy is both simple and daring. It hinges on a complete integration of structure and services in the long-span barrel-vaulted roof under which the whole building shelters, permanently in shadow, letting in indirect daylight without solar gain. The roof floats above the floorplates to form a deliberate separation of shell and structure. This applies equally to the skin and services, emphasised by the cladding and internal partitions – which stop short of the roof with only clear glass rising within the curvature of the vaults – and by the service cores located externally on the north and south elevations, which rise only to the same horizontal datum as the cladding.

The difference between the two buildings is that Boots is both

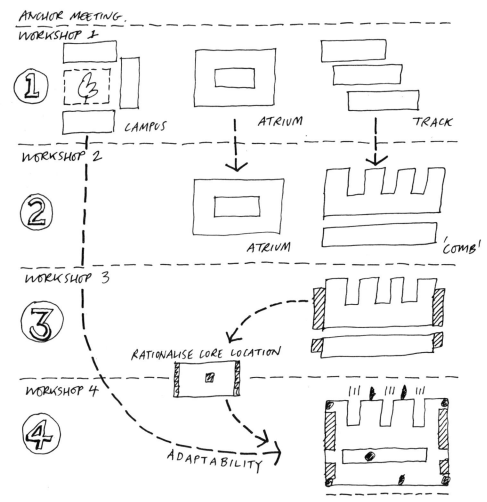

ANCHOR MEETING.
WORKSHOP 1

① CAMPUS

ATRIUM

TRACK

WORKSHOP 2

②

ATRIUM

'COMB'

WORKSHOP 3

③

RATIONALISE CORE LOCATION

WORKSHOP 4

④

ADAPTABILITY

The plan of the new building was arrived at after intensive study of a wide range of options. Three possible models were analysed, costed and value engineered, with the final plan taking the best parts of each to secure the most adaptable workspace.

a generic shed and a floorplate model. Apicorp, by being so much more 'integrated', is more highly engineered and specific. Boots relies much less on its structural ingenuity and display. It eschews the current preference for exposed concrete as a radiant source, and as a means of architectural expression. Instead, chilled ceiling panels are used throughout for comfort cooling.

It is, above all, a solution derived directly from DEGW's earlier experience of refurbishing the DTI headquarters. Mixed-mode buildings have not reconciled entirely the different comfort conditions experienced at the perimeter of a building and deeper within the floorplate, although recent advances in building management systems are constantly improving user control.

The environmental consequence of the deep plan is that a wide range of different uses can be accommodated. In the climatically-dependent perimeter zones, external influences can cause relatively large fluctuations in heating and cooling loads. These are locally controlled: in Apicorp, with re-circulating fan-coil units in the floor void, and at Boots with induction units integrated into the spandrel beneath the window. The deep-plan zones in both buildings, how-

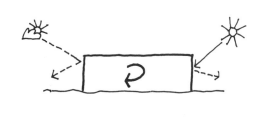

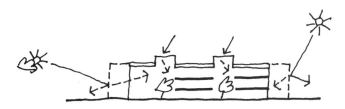

The atria in the building act as thermal modulators, encouraging the circulation of air and helping to regulate solar gain. Service cores are pushed to the ends of the block to provide unencumbered workspace.

The 'comb' plan of the final layout, with its atria and fire stairs penetrating the office floors, allows the future subdivision of the building.

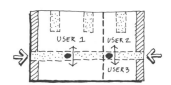

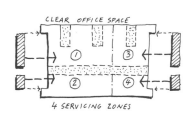

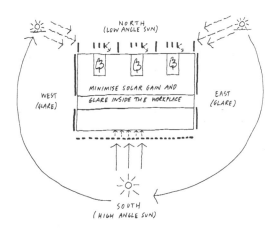

129

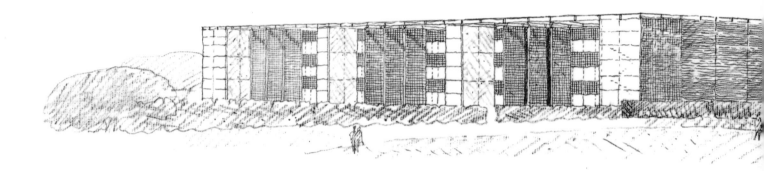

The heavily tex-
tured exterior of
the new build-
ing, contrasting
with the sleek-
ness of the SOM
original, reflects
a new-genera-
tion approach to
energy conser-
vation. External
screen walls on
the long east
and west eleva-
tions control
solar gain and
provide a uni-
form external
look, regardless
of what is going
on behind.

ever, are not affected by the external environment and are condition-
ed by the standard displacement-
ventilation systems.

Boots differs from recent low-
energy buildings in the UK in that
it is sealed, it does not exploit pas-
sive solar gain, nor does it balance
the admittance of sunlight with
thermal gain. Yet its credentials
are no less 'environmentally correct'. Boots keeps out the sun to
avoid exceeding the limitations of
the chilled panels, which are set
at a few degrees below room tem-
perature. It does so in the same
way Apicorp does, with louvres
and solid cores, except that the
orientation of louvred and solid
facades is reversed: the cores at
Boots are on the east and west
elevations, with louvres to the
north and south; Apicorp's louvres

are on the east and west, with the
cores north and south. In both
buildings, shell, structure, services,
scenery and setting are legible,
each able to respond independently to its own life cycle and rate of
change.

In the Apicorp building the
large central, oval and part daylit
courtyard is a focus for organisation and circulation as well as being the principal lung for the building. Looking up to the underside
of the roof vaults, the sides of the
oval rooflights carved into the
double-skin barrel vaults contain
the return-air grilles. The rooflights
are deep enough, with their external screening, to admit only first
or second reflections, not direct
sunlight even though it is virtual-
ly overhead. These rooflights are
repeated over the smaller courtyards as, in the Boots building,

A regular distri-
bution of escape
stairs and atria
ensures circula-
tion through the
building is kept
as simple as
possible.

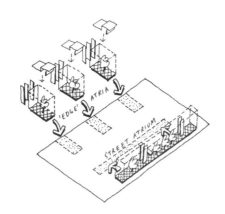

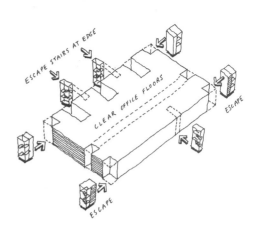

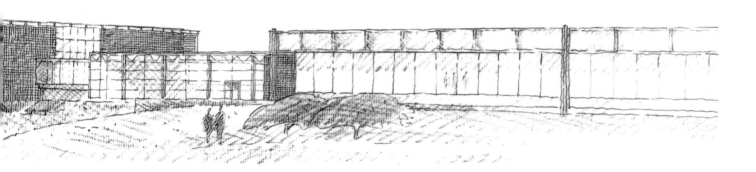

The elevation is
a major advance
over standards
prevailing in the
1960s. Instead
of creating envi-
ronmental prob-
lems, the layer-
ed facade of the
new building has
been designed
to combat them.

are the north lights, inset into the
long-span roof together with their
continuous return-air grilles.

Another part of the low-energy strategy of both buildings is
the design of the skin which, in
each case, rejects the two favour-
ite elements in the curtain wall
vocabulary; full-height glazing in all
its variants and in-board perimeter
columns. Solid spandrels are used
instead – for the thermal mass of
their upstands, to keep the heat
out, to hide unsightly clutter, and
to provide a solid edge to work
up against. Perimeter columns are
incorporated into the external walls
of both buildings. In Apicorp they
are contained within the overall
depth of the deep but lightweight
wall construction which helps to
modulate the penetration of light,

The layout of workplaces around the atria is intended to encourage team-working, while retaining scope for quiet areas and private meeting rooms.

The perimeter atria of the new Boots building provide points of focus within an otherwise deep plan, helping to form local neighbourhoods, each with their own identity.

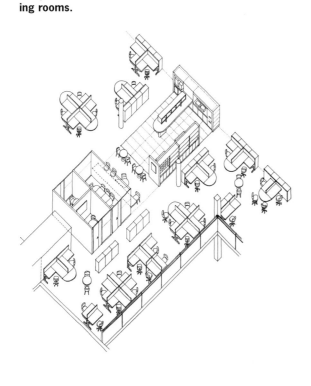

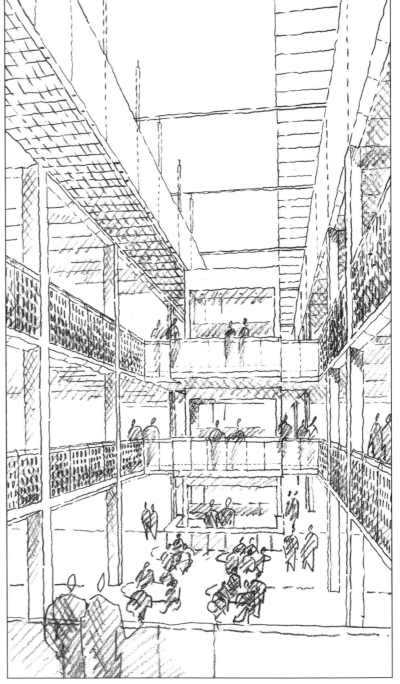

Engineered to control light and solar gain, the precast-concrete roof vaults of the Apicorp building generate their own powerful language, both inside and out.

while a similar solution at Boots allows the installation of partitions and workspaces right up to the window sill – the very antithesis of the SOM building where the perimeter can only be used for circulation.

In Boots the spandrel elevations are clad with replaceable, dry, rain-screen tiles. In Apicorp these tiles are of local marble and are fixed to the wall flush with the double-glazed window units. There is a chequered pattern of smaller windows at eye level while larger ones above these reflect light off the ceilings to simulate the visual texture of traditional Middle Eastern tiling.

Boots is dry-clad in an industrialised proprietary terracotta tile system in an angled frame, cold-bridge-free reinterpretation of the steel and brick vernacular of the Mies van der Rohe buildings at the Illinois Institute of Technology – a contextual counterpoint to the adjacent SOM building with its classic 'Crown Hall' resonance. The iconography of the two buildings is derived neither from form nor surface, but from a deep understanding of both light and air, and of how workplaces are utilised. The two buildings respond to their very different contexts using the same underlying building form and cladding principles.

The Apicorp building avoids entirely the pastiche of Middle Eastern styles often adopted by Western architects. The vaults and columns can be read as references to more than one architectural tradition, but they have provided the client with the strong image it sought.

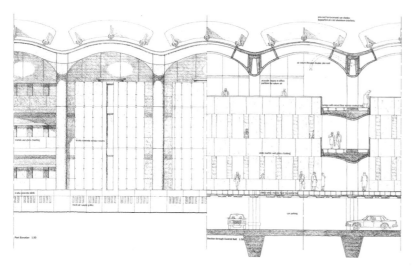

Parking is provided underground. The concrete columns and arches provide a powerful framework for the office floors, which are screened by heavy marble cladding.

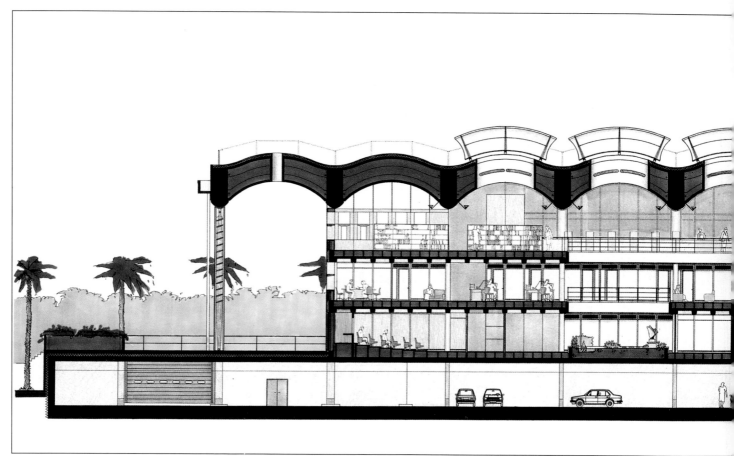

A long section through the Apicorp building, showing its relationship to an adjacent housing project that takes the form of a pyramid.

Cross Section A-A

The overall rationale of the Apicorp headquarters is explained in this presentation section. The roof is a massive and dense shelter, almost independent of the office floors below. The offices themselves surround a large central courtyard and four smaller atria, all lit by generous rooflights above.

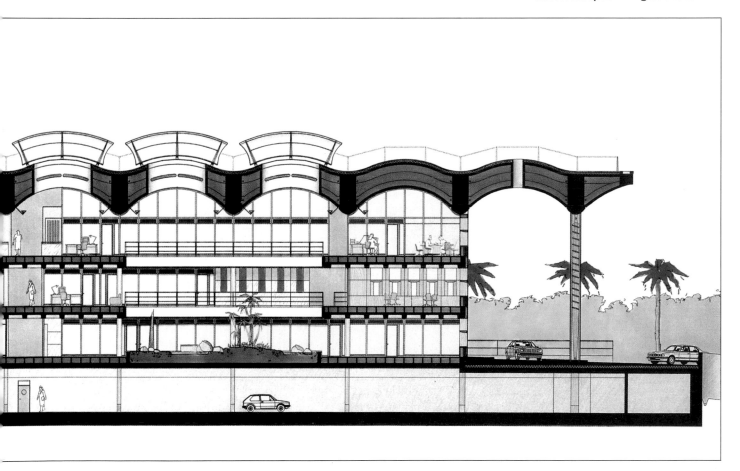

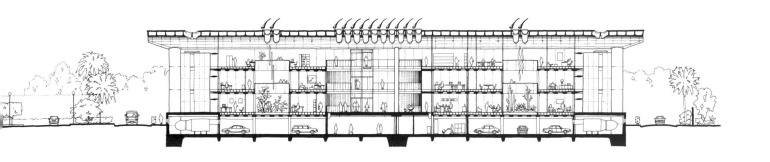

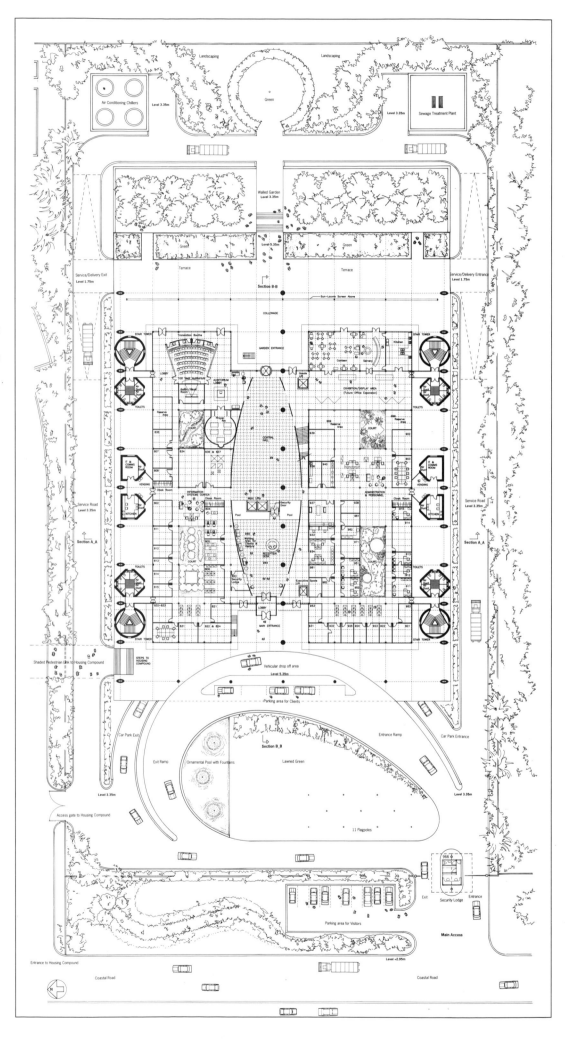

The Apicorp plan is highly rational and draws on the Modern tradition for its clear servicing and circulation strategy. Staircases and lavatories are banished to the perimeter along the east and west elevations, where they also provide solar screening for the facade.

Organisationally, Apicorp and Boots are worlds apart. One is 90 per cent cellular, the other 90 per cent open plan. No one in Boots will have a private office, although everyone is expected to have an assigned 'home-base'. Bookable quiet rooms and meeting rooms will be part of a regime of shared and team-working spaces which must be capable of change overnight. Apicorp, on the other hand, has been planned initially with a large number of cellular offices, though in such a way as to allow organisational change later in its life. Both buildings could accommodate hives suitable for large working groups, a cellular layout like Apicorp's, small group-working and project dens, or the more radical desk-less club spaces.

Above all, both buildings are designed inside and out to provide places for interaction. Collective spaces are at the heart of each. These spaces are neither voids, nor are they fully-occupied workplaces in the conventional, highly supervised way of old-fashioned offices. They are socially and organisationally cohesive. They demonstrate that it is still possible to emulate the power of the Larkin Building or of Wright's other office masterpiece for Johnson Wax at Racine, Wisconsin. But they also show that it is the combination of the place-making power of archi-

tecture – first, with an understanding of light and air and, second, with a firm grasp of how best to accommodate changing patterns of work – that is the key to the design of the new generation of office buildings.

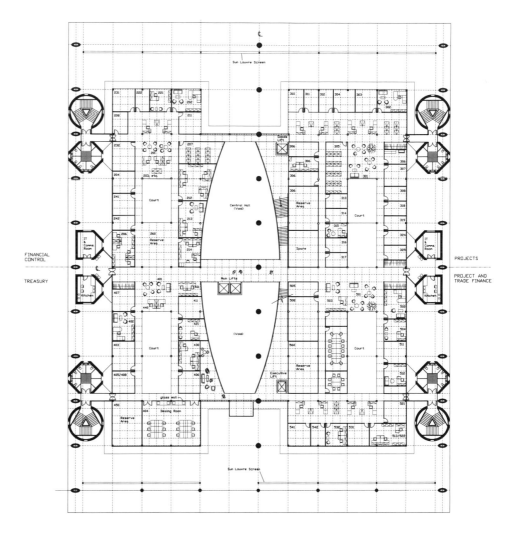

In essence, the Apicorp plan is a typical DEGW three-zone layout, two pavilions separated by a great central atrium. The floors are laid out on a regular 1.5 x 1.5 metre grid to accommodate a range of office types and other support spaces.

The architecture
of the building
emerges from
the plan and the
section with no
obviously rheto-
rical additions.
The building is
monumental but
not ostentatious.

The drama of
the building is
intensified by the
devices needed
to ensure envi-
ronmental com-
fort, not least
the great solar
'sails' on the
roof. Fabricat-
ed from translu-
cent white sail-
cloth stretched
over curved
frames, these
protect the roof-
lights and the
spaces below
from direct sun-
light.

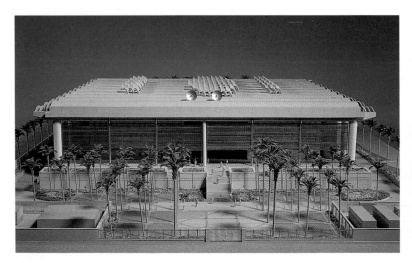

DEGW's new
Apicorp build-
ing successfully
merges Western
and Middle East-
ern traditions to
create a mem-
orable fusion.

139

Regeneration

The history of the last hundred years of city planning and architecture can be interpreted as a growing schism with the past. The Modern Movement deliberately broke with older perceptions of space and social order. The traditional concept of space – static, sequential and closed – was superseded by attempts to create new kinds of space that were fluid, variable and open. Spatially complex mixes of use were reduced to single function zones to make everything of equal status. Contrast was valued more than continuity to accentuate 'the shock of the new'. The distinction between the public and the private realm was exaggerated. Isolated objects were placed in space and the spaces within and between buildings were sharply differentiated.

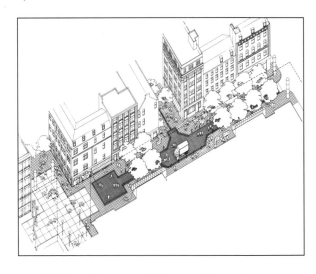

A detail from DEGW's urban masterplan for Merchant City, Glasgow. The scheme was based on using existing resources wherever possible.

Today things are different. There is a new willingness among architects and planners to embrace rather than to reject the past. Spatial and temporal continuity is again in vogue. New processes in urban planning, design and management are mending at least some of the fractures listed above by addressing the importance of the continuity of inside and out, by reinventing the

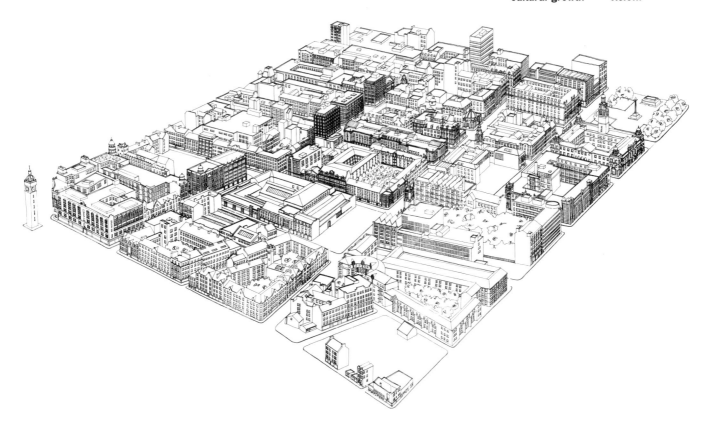

The area plan for Merchant City was seen as an operational framework to accommodate cultural growth and commercial change, not a static masterplan expressing a complete architectural vision.

use of time, space and ownership and by re-establishing the importance of widespread popular participation in planning the agenda for the future. DEGW has played an important part in this shift, adapting as many spaces between buildings as inside them, in a variety of roles that extend from space planning to urban planning.

Masterplans were popular with the architects and planners of the Modern Movement. Conceived as complete entities, it was invariably assumed that such plans would be implemented by single bodies over relatively short periods of time. They were much stronger as visions of the final product than as programmes of implementation.

In a rapidly changing world, masterplans now have a very different meaning. They have become flexible master strategies, distinguished by a new

focus on process and continuity, rather than static masterplans. To DEGW a masterplan now means a physical and operational framework within which change can be accommodated and development is incremental.

Two examples will begin to explain what this change means. The first is DEGW's masterplan for the Merchant City in Glasgow, the urban-planning framework for the regeneration of the city's historic market quarter, adjacent to the main shopping concourse of Buchanan Street and within walking distance of the University of Strathclyde campus, the commercial area of St Enoch's and the old business centre of the city. The management consultants, McKinsey, and the planner,

Gordon Cullen, had already identified the area in their 1986 study, *Vision for Glasgow Action*, as a potential creative quarter for the city centre.

DEGW's masterplan built incrementally on what already existed. A comprehensive analysis of the vacant and under-utilised sites and buildings in the area came first. These were then classified according to the potential of the types of space they provided, to suggest opportunities for new or more intensive uses. In parallel, an audit was carried out of the area's human potential – the organisations and individuals who might be catalytic in its development.

The area had been seen by planning policymakers as slow to change despite having absorbed considerable grant aid. A single drawing was prepared which identified both completed and proposed projects. At one stroke the neighbourhood was shown to be on the move. Perceptions were changed and new opportunities were seized. A series of small schemes, undertaken by a combination of private and public investment, is the means by which the masterplan is being achieved.

The characteristics of the Merchant City masterplan are that:
–   it is based on existing physical and human resources, adding new buildings only if they enhance the social and business potential of the existing stock. Stock-taking has identified a huge variety of existing spaces from small rooms in residential buildings to large open areas in the market halls and in Goldberg's department store;
–   it identifies key projects where public investment is most likely to stimulate private sector involvement. For example, a pedestrian area composed of a sequence of public and semi-public spaces flowing within and between buildings was proposed to enhance the potential for creative re-use of the redundant Sheriffs' Courts, Clydesdale Bank and Goldberg's department store;
–   it stimulates the local economy by providing a rich mix of businesses, accommodation types and development approaches. DEGW's 'premises ladder' matches the needs of businesses at each stage of their development with suitable premises and leases;

Inherent in the contrast between the Ralph Agas Plan of London, of 1570, and Le Corbusier's Modern Movement vision for Paris, of 1925, is the dichotomy between what to preserve and what to tear down. After the Modernist experiment, DEGW, like others, is learning what to retain and what to reinvent in planning the modern city.

— it establishes a flexible development pro-gramme with measurable milestones for flexible implementation responding to the changing economy and to the availability of public funds. A variety of investment paths means that the whole development will not be held up if any single decision is delayed;

— proposes a menu of projects from larger scale investments such as the establishment of the pedestrian precinct to low-cost initiatives such as co-ordinated graphics and 'street dressing' that can be undertaken indepen-dently of long-term decisions and yet have an immediate impact;

— and supports local champions and estab-lishes a local area development forum to raise expectations, to attract resources and to sustain local interest and energy.

Much of what is proposed in *Vision for the Merchant City* has still to be achieved. However, it is the masterplan that matters – the strategic framework for seizing opportunities that can be implemented as demand catches up with supply.

Aerial view of the Carl Zeiss factory at Jena prior to regeneration. The new masterplan needed to evolve within a rapidly changing context.

The second example is in Germany. In contrast to the gradual metamorphosis of Glasgow's Merchant City, the changes initiated in the German city of Jena have been much more explosive. With German reunification and the collapse of the Soviet-style 'command' economy, cities in the East needed instant strategies for economic restructuring and physical revival. Jena was typical: a city of 100,000 inhabitants totally dependent on a historic university and a single business, Carl Zeiss, the famous optics firm. The physical core of the city was symbolically dominated by the Carl Zeiss factory and the 1960s university tower.

The Carl Zeiss optical works has played a central role in the life of Jena since 1846.

Werksansicht aus dem Jahre 1896
Das Verwaltungsgebäude war gerade fertiggestellt. Links neben dem Verwaltungsgebäude steht das Wohnhaus Carl Zeiß, rechts das Gebäude, das 1888 gebaut, 1891 und 1896 zum dargestellten Gebäude erweitert und für den Neubau des Bau 1C wieder abgerissen wurde.

Carl Zeiss, Optische Werkstaette, Jena.
1846 1896.
Archiv B.10963

Given the new pressures of the 'market' economy the challenge facing Jena in 1991 was to:
– change the vertically-organised Carl Zeiss enterprise into a modern, much more sharply focused, core business with a network of independent, supporting suppliers;
– shift to a mixed economy with a variety of retailing opportunities;

– ensure that the knowledge base of the university could become the catalyst for retraining and change for the benefit of the city as a whole;
– and attract external investment.

DEGW's masterplanning approach, as in Glasgow, was first to understand and then to exploit the qualities of the space that already existed and to relate what exists to the changing economy and pattern of demand. The result was proposals for a mixed programme of new building and refurbishment that could be achieved at different speeds and in different sequences. A critically important programme of public events was used to celebrate the return of the introverted and inaccessible Hauptwerkstadt, the old centre of the Carl Zeiss works, to public use.

Within five years, through a continuing programme of physical, economic and educational restructuring, the entire centre of the city has been revitalised. The 'works' street has been opened and glazed over to become a new focus for the city. New investment and new construction have attracted the university – and many other activities – to the site. The new Jena shows the value of a clear vision, flexible guidelines and a coherent framework in marshalling opportunities without hindering enterprise.

The methodologies of 'supply and demand' that match a company's pattern of work to its building resources are well established in DEGW's approach to commercial space planning. The same approach provides equally valuable tools for establishing masterplans in urban areas. Old-fashioned planners had attempted to superimpose abstract constructs of use and zoning on local areas with small regard for the real uses that

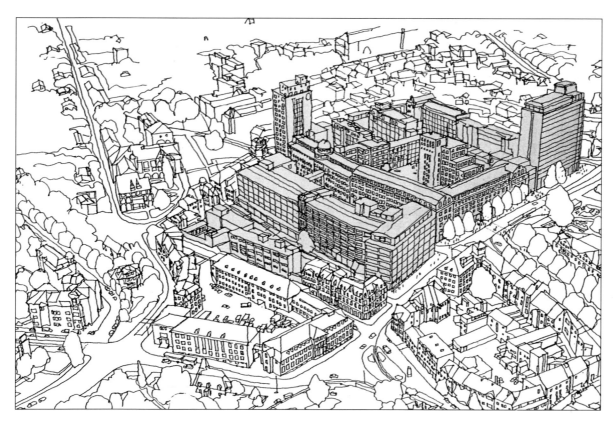

already existed or for the quality of the built fabric as it actually was. The result was the 'sweep-the-slate-clean' approach of comprehensive redevelopment.

The best example in London was Covent Garden in the early 1970s, struggling to survive despite the 'grand slam' planning vision of the planning authority, the Greater London Council. DEGW, working closely with the economic and planning consultants URBED and applying to urban planning tools adapted from space planning, surveyed the intricate network of the local economy as well as the physical characteristics and the patterns of use of the existing building stock. The results were illuminating – economically as well as politically. While an articulate population of 3000 lived in Covent Garden,

nearly 30,000 other people worked there but had precious little say on plans for the future of an area that was critically important to them. In addition, it became clear that the economic well-being of Covent Garden depended upon a complex web of uses for which comprehensive redevelopment would certainly be fatal.

Around the Royal Opera House were – and still are – the button makers, seamstresses, timber merchants, theatrical agents, restaurateurs, printers and graphic artists, a hard to classify variety of interests and uses, but all vital to the success of the Opera. The space available in Covent Garden remains perfect for mixed use with larger retail, workshop and office spaces on lower floors

At Willow House, London, DEGW's radical refurbishment of the upper floors and the addition of a new roof has transformed a mundane 1950s building.

combined with smaller attic spaces above that are so suitable for small apartments and studios. DEGW and URBED's early work in Covent Garden, put forward in 1976, established a methodology for urban stock-taking – for matching physical supply and social demand, that was to be more comprehensively applied in charting the future of Hackney and Islington in the early 1980s.

The techniques of taking stock are essential to an urban-planning process that is capable of building on what already exists. Healthy cities provide continuity with the past, drawing on existing physical and organisational strengths. The competition brief for London's South Bank is a more recent example of DEGW's ability to use carefully structured workshops and focus groups to allow the many and varied parties involved in complex

DEGW's competition brief for the redevelopment of London's South Bank showed the value of focus groups in reconciling conflicting interests.

South Bank Centre   STRATEGIC BRIEF FOR MASTER PLANNER SELECTION

networks to establish a picture of what they really want – matching multifarious interests, artistic and commercial, against both the existing stock of space and the development opportunities that design imagination can create.

As the pace of change increases, so the need for local distinctiveness becomes more important. Managing continuity means respecting what is best from the past and adding appropriate space

and technology to meet emerging social and organisational needs. DEGW's regeneration of warehouses at Rotherhithe (1974-82), under the development direction of URBED, not only created, step by step, a lively mixture of living, working and leisure facilities, but also anticipated the much larger scale – and not always so sensitive – reconstruction of the rest of London's Docklands in the 1980s and '90s.

At Rotherhithe minimal financial resources combined with the imagination and effort of pioneering incomers made it possible to adapt old buildings to new uses and new technology. The same energy, talent and user involvement have also made Rotherhithe a very special and distinctive place, easily recognised within the surrounding morass of expensive, waterside redevelopment.

As might be expected, DEGW's own office at Porters North in King's Cross, London, which was built in 1904 as a warehouse and bottling plant to supply thirsty Edwardian London with beer, has been skilfully converted to meet the needs of late twentieth-century knowledge work. Today, the DEGW offices are seen as an exemplar of 'new ways of working', while the building itself has become a catalyst for the revival of the surrounding area.

Organisational invention, it can be argued, has outstripped the inventiveness of planners and architects to create new locations and settings to accommodate changing needs. The implication is that the central design challenge for the future is to design new settings for new purposes.

DEGW and Twijnstra Gudde are currently addressing this challenge on a very large scale at Utrecht, in the Randstadt region of the Netherlands, which is facing the challenge of re-inventing

Porters North, near King's Cross, was built in 1904 as a bottling plant. Now DEGW's London headquarters, it is a successful example of recycling an old building and regenerating a locality.

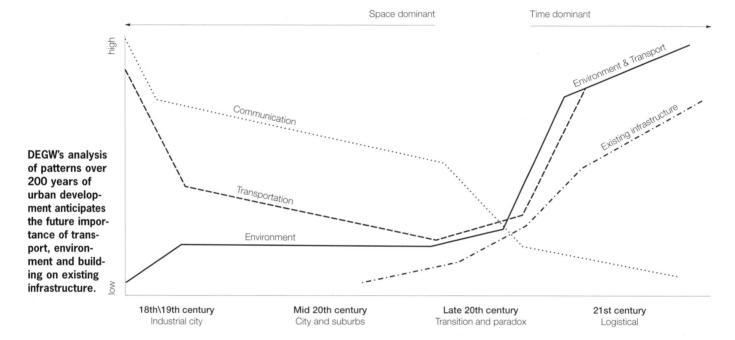

Space dominant   Time dominant

high

Communication

DEGW's analysis of patterns over 200 years of urban development anticipates the future importance of transport, environment and building on existing infrastructure.

Environment & Transport

Existing infrastructure

Transportation

Environment

low

18th\19th century	Mid 20th century	Late 20th century	21st century
Industrial city	City and suburbs	Transition and paradox	Logistical

itself. The city has two key development sites. The first is the Central Station area where a throughput of 75 million passengers annually is predicted by the year 2000. The station will have direct rail links to Germany, Belgium, France and the UK, and is particularly well located in the Randstadt because Utrecht's busy and beautiful historic core is a mere 22 minutes from the airport at Schipol.

The second site at the edge of the same city is being planncd to accommodate 1500 housing units and over 300,000 square metres of office and other business and support space. This site will be within 10 minutes of the centre of Utrecht by light rail as well as adjacent to two major motorways. Both sites, though independent, can be linked to exploit synergies between the two – one will be internationally biased given its excellent connections and amenities, while the other

will be more attractive regionally because of its superior car access and parking and lower costs. It is DEGW and Twijnstra Gudde's task to invent a masterplan that will help Utrecht make maximum use of these different and complementary facilities in the rapidly-changing European property market.

Technology has the ability not only to shrink distance but to shrink space. The faded glory of Piccadilly Circus and the Edwardian elegance of the Trocadero have been rejuvenated by the introduction of the technology of Sega World where all the bare knuckle thrills of a theme park are concentrated into a two-metre square experience of virtual reality. New technologies will stimulate lateral thinking and lateral thinking will lead to new paradigms of use. Redundant buildings will have even more potential to accommodate new

Below: the 1958 Lloyd's Building was refurbished by DEGW following the corporation's expansion into its new headquarters.

uses as we learn to make modern technology and old buildings co-exist.

Diversity makes cities healthy. Central to DEGW's current programming and design thinking is the necessity of accepting and balancing conflicting interests. The challenge is to provide solutions that can accommodate 'both . . and' rather than 'either . . or'. DEGW's research for IBM in the 1970s – which analysed open-plan offices in four European countries – showed that it was not so much that enclosed offices were intrinsically good or open offices bad, but rather that for all members of staff there exists a tension between personal desires and corporate expectations which different kinds of office design can, in certain circumstances, exacerbate. The ideal design solution balances the corporate advantages of interaction and increased communication with the end-users' personal preferences for a degree of privacy and an opportunity to express their individual identity.

Just as workplace settings at the micro level should be designed to accommodate different user pressures so, at the macro level, the city of the twenty-first century is likely to become a series of 'nodes' of intense activity – linked by air, wheels and the latest telecommunications to provide, for each individual, a huge and diverse portfolio of locations and settings appropriate for increasingly

The virtuality of Sega World is transforming the faded Edwardian elegance of Piccadilly Circus, as time becomes more dominant than space.

varied activities. Saltaire, on the edge of industrial Bradford, epitomises such a centre. This model industrial community has been gradually converted into a place for living and leisure as well as for working. Within the abundant floor space of Salt Mills the owner, Jonathan Silver, has created three floors of retailing, restaurants and art galleries. Saltaire, through creative planning and inspired marketing, has been made into a very special destination.

Similarly, at the Babelsberg Film Studios to the south of Berlin, a new centre is being established that reflects changing media technologies. Babelsberg was the pre-war Mecca of the German

film industry and continued to be the media centre for the Communist regime. Today, the generous site that was required for a vertically integrated industry, which accommodated everything from making costumes to processing film, can be shrunk by a third and, indeed, will continue to shrink as a result of computer animation. DEGW was commissioned in 1995 to review the competition-winning masterplan by testing it, appropriately enough, against alternative scenarios of change. The result is a strategic brief expressing alternative visions of what a 'media city' could be like. The new Babelsberg is intended not just to recall the pre-war film empire but to be a place for

Saltaire, on the outskirts of Bradford in northern England, as it was in the mid-nineteenth century. It suffered a prolonged period of industrial decline before its imaginative regeneration as a place for living and leisure, as well as work, in the 1980s.

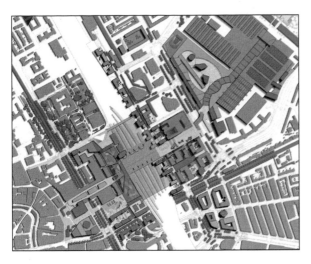

DEGW and Twijnstra Gudde's masterplan for Utrecht focuses on the area near the central station, now one of Europe's most important international gateways.

living, working and relaxing and to attract emerging, independent, high-technology creative businesses.

Such lasting and successful solutions must be the result of a combination of a clear vision, client and user involvement and imaginative design. Ideas for solving complex problems are most likely to emerge when there is intense discussion across disciplines and between experts and users. Masterplanning depends upon such processes. The Urban Design Group (UDG), which Worthington chaired, has long championed the cause of 'Action Planning'.

At the two Highbury Initiative events run by DEGW and URBED in the early 1980s, Birmingham City Council brought together experts from the UK, Europe, Japan and North America to rethink the future of Birmingham's city core. What has transformed Birmingham is the result of these two events breaking the deadlock between conflicting interest groups. Other similarly intensive events in Manchester, Southwark and Wakefield have, through careful preparation and the selective use of external skills, helped communities to establish their goals and to masterplan their futures.

Design has a vital role in this new interpretation of masterplanning. Yet urban design is a skill that has all but disappeared from most city planning departments. The designer's role can only be reintroduced if value is shown to be added. Designers, working with the community, on their feet, acting as animators and facilitators, must be able to articulate opportunities through a thorough analysis and critique of what exists, to set goals and establish visions, and to communicate opportunities, facilitate action and help diverse interest groups share a common vision.

What distinguishes architecture from building is the meaningful and elegant allocation of

Saltaire today, complete with restaurants, art galleries, workshops and studios. An old industrial community has been skilfully marketed to attract new visitors.

available resources to social purposes. Good design must add value, must improve the quality of life. Consequently, the process of masterplanning described above is inherently political. It is designed to inspire the community to own the city and make their own places within the city not just better but memorable. DEGW began by trying to understand the use and the planning of spaces within buildings. The same processes and similar insights have been applied at the hugely ambitious scale of urban design through a new definition of masterplanning. The future quality of the city centres of Glasgow, Birmingham, Jena, and Utrecht will, it is hoped, justify the venture.

151

Reviving Jena

DEGW's concern for the workplace extends from the placing of a desk to the regeneration of an entire city district. Regeneration was an early theme in the practice's work. It argued the case for re-using redundant industrial buildings in northern England and New England and was in at the beginning of the 'workspace' movement of the 1970s – the progenitor of revival in the once-forlorn factory and warehousing belts around the fringe of central London and other big cities. When Covent Garden ceased to be the centre of London's fruit and vegetable market, it faced dismemberment for road schemes and redevelopment. Even when the area was reprieved, the question remained: for whom and for what should it be regenerated? There was only a very small resident population but DEGW's role in voicing the concerns of the 'working community' – mainly small firms, often quite new – was crucial in shaping the area's future.

Work for the Department of the Environment on the future of disused warehouse and factory space in Hackney followed. "There was a quite staggering lack of imagination in those days", says John Worthington. "The development system couldn't cope with anything but new buildings." DEGW cultivated links with organisations like URBED and with community activists, taking inspiration from the work of Jane Jacobs, Christopher Alexander and other theorists whom Worthington and Francis Duffy had become familiar with during their sojourn in the USA. It was a matter of 'stocktaking the city', measuring its resources and assessing their potential value in terms of investment and jobs. The approach was applied, for example, in Glasgow's Merchant City, then a run-down fringe of near-dereliction.

In the 1970s, it was customary for developers and community groups to regard each other with open hostility on the assumption that their interests were inherently in conflict. But in Hackney, the local (Labour-controlled) authority was desperate to encourage developers to cross the City boundary into Shoreditch. DEGW's notion of 'collaborative development', backed by Stanhope, underpinned the workshops it ran for local activists and councillors, developers and investors, with the object of envisaging how development could be beneficial to all parties. The massive Broadgate office scheme burst across the City boundary and DEGW found itself heavily involved in briefing studies for the new dealing floors then heavily in demand, late twentieth-century equivalents of the market buildings of the Victorian era.

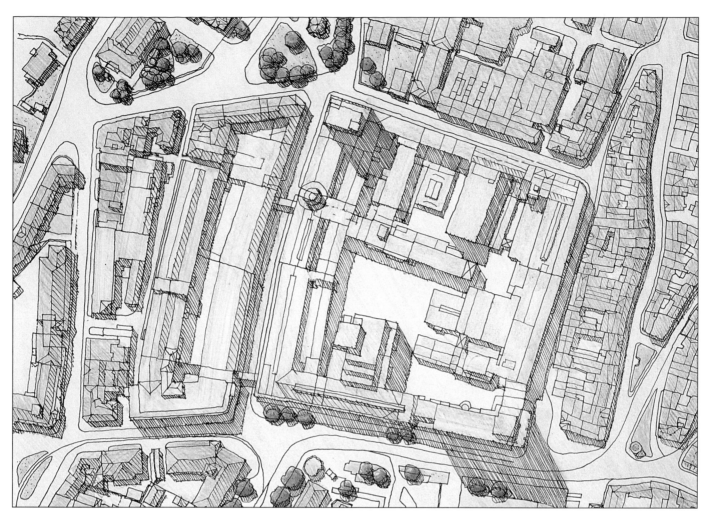

DEGW's masterplan for the Carl Zeiss works at Jena addressed issues which were central to the city in the aftermath of German reunification.

The Zeiss works was, in every sense, central to Jena and the masterplan had to knit the finished complex into the life of the city.

John Worthington sees cities as places of perpetual change, closely reflecting an ever-changing economy. Broadgate exemplified the change from the old manufacturing economy to one based on financial services, part of a global market. Change is inevitable, but it needs to be planned and controlled if the social fabric is to stand. DEGW's recent involvement in the former East Germany involved working at the cutting edge of change.

Since German re-unification in 1990, the former East has been subjected to the forces of world competition – unemployment has rocketed and supporting the former DDR has placed strains even on the huge German economy. The great Carl Zeiss works at Jena, founded by Carl Zeiss a century and a half ago, was the pride of the DDR, having been meticulously rebuilt after wartime devastation as the prime manufacturer of

optical equipment in the Eastern bloc. It was known throughout the world as a manufacturer of planetariums. As recently as the 1985, Zeiss employed over 30,000 people in Jena – a town of only 100,000 inhabitants – with another 30,000 employees elsewhere in East Germany. The firm was heavily tied to the Soviet war machine and insulated from Western competition – including that from the rival Zeiss works established in the West after 1945.

With the collapse of the Soviet Union and the DDR, total ruin loomed for Jena. Philip Tidd of DEGW recalls early visits to the works, soon after re-unification, and seeing craftsmen lovingly polishing lenses by hand. "It was low-tech, survivalist, quaint", he says. "But it was clear that it couldn't compete on the world scene. Zeiss and Jena had to adapt or die." Jena

A number of the buildings on the site merited retention and conversion within the masterplan. This 1912 block has been incorporated into an otherwise new hotel.

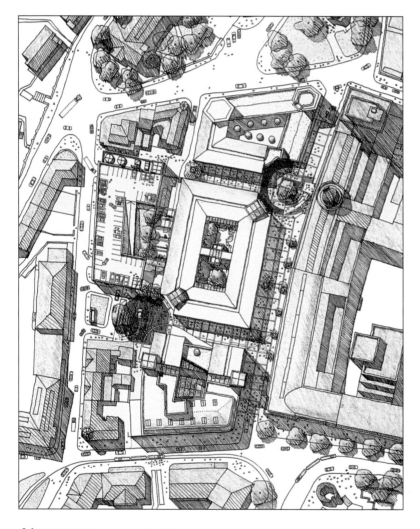

A key concept was the introduction of new routes through the site, previously an enclosed 'fortress' with no public access. A central spine road provided the most significant new pedestrian thoroughfare – initially it was intended to remain open to the sky.

itself is a remarkable place, with a highly-educated population and a famous university, and it had no intention of dying. But the shock of Zeiss's collapse struck hard: 30,000 people lost their jobs when the firm went bankrupt and another 20,000 were laid off in 1992 by the new public trust that had taken over control of its operations. In Jena, only 3000 staff were retained on a satellite site. Four other factories, including the historic town centre plant, were closed down. The collapse was traumatic, but it was actually a re-run – though much accelerated – of the collapse of manufacturing in British cities during the 1970s and '80s.

The political context of reunification, however, provided a benevolent funding regime to cushion the potential victims of change. Large sums of federal cash were poured into the region of Thuringia to retrain the unemployed and foster new investment: nobody doubts that Jena will be a highly successful player among twenty-first century German towns and it is already being promoted as 'the high-tech centre at the heart of Germany'. JenOptik, the new company set up to run the old Zeiss business, was headed up by Lothar Späth, sometime prime minister of Baden-Württemberg – where he had been James Stirling's client for the Stuttgart Staatsgalerie.

154

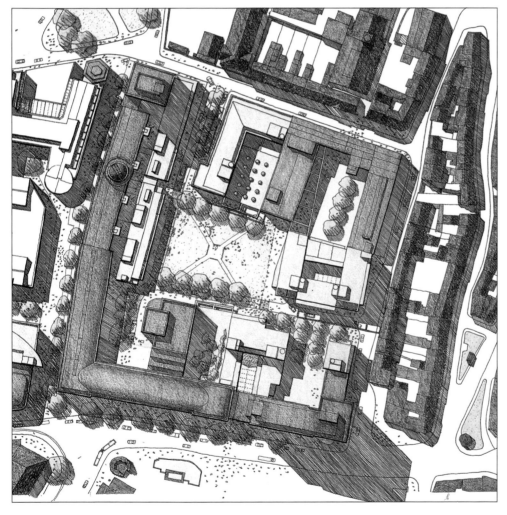

The redevelopment of the site included the demolition of some existing buildings to create a breathing space for fresh uses, including a new central square.

Selective clearance of the northern part of the site allowed for the retention of the best existing buildings.

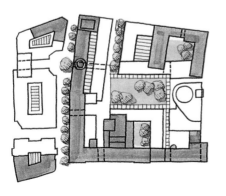
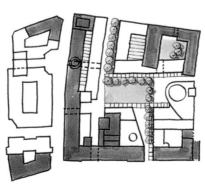
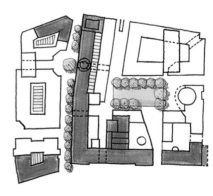

155

DEGW's earliest
proposals includ-
ed a new central
square with car
parking below.

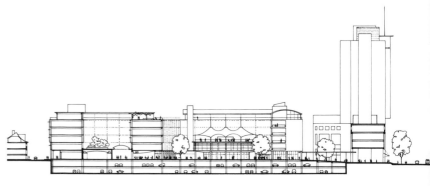

JenOptik faced the mammoth
task of retraining displaced workers and finding a use for its redundant buildings. The two objectives
went hand in hand. Although the
suburban sites were mostly sold
off for redevelopment, part of the
historic town centre works (the
Hauptwerk) was pressed into use
as seminar rooms and training
facilities. The future of this site was
clearly critical for Jena. Among
the many buildings were a number
protected for their historic interest.

But, as Philip Tidd explains, the
path of regeneration was not clear.
"There was absolutely no established local market", he says.

Tidd had been responsible for
launching DEGW's Berlin office:
"We would have liked to work from
Jena itself but in those days it
was impossible", he recalls. "Getting an international telephone line

The new public
thoroughfare
helped open up
for re-use the
best of the ex-
isting buildings
at the heart of
the site.

DEGW saw the central square as a major new local amenity created out of a dense tangle of buildings. In its final form, the square has become a popular meeting place for young and old alike, many from the technical university which now occupies a large part of the site.

157

The best of the existing buildings have been refurbished for a wide range of new uses.

An interim proposal exploring the possibility of glazing over the central thoroughfare.

The different geometries between the new and old wings of the hotel have been cleverly resolved with a dramatic full-height atrium.

could take hours!" Some West German consultants had looked at the Zeiss site and concluded that total clearance was the best answer. "We had to prove the value of every building we wanted to keep", says Tidd. In the end, 60 per cent of the buildings were retained, though there was no question that the changes on the site would need to be far-reaching. There were 10 hectares of closely-packed blocks, a walled fortress at the centre of the town. The oldest dated from the 1890s, the newest from around 1960. The buildings included the oldest reinforced-concrete structures in Germany. Building 29 was a much admired 1929 block by Emil Fahrenkamp, while the 'Hochhaus', a landmark 1930s tower block, provided a strong marker for the site. There had to be sacrifices to open up space for change, but the general prescription was one of conservation and adaptation.

DEGW's commission to draw up a masterplan for the Hauptwerk came in 1991, when the buildings there were vacant and facing dereliction. The client was supportive of a very extensive process of consultation with the local community: there were fears about the future but an acceptance of change – and a degree of real optimism.

Creating a development brief was not easy. Even though the final mix of new uses remained unclear, the brief had to define immediate,

medium- and long-term uses for many of the existing buildings, while retaining an in-built flexibility. However, it was fairly clear what Jena lacked after nearly half a century of Communism: service industries, small businesses in general and space to house them, restaurants, hotels and modern office space. Much of this could be provided on the Hauptwerk site, which was ideally located to act as the new 'heart' of the town. DEGW

Seen from above or below, the new 140-metre long galleria is the most striking feature of the entire scheme.

The form of the galleria roof is essentially that of a lean-to, supported by one of the refurbished buildings.

identified the West German town of Erlangen as an example. It was of similar size, also possessed a highly-regarded university, and was dominated by one company, in this case the electrical giant Siemens. The most obvious contrast lay in Erlangen's wealth of small businesses and of cultural and leisure amenities, the product of decades of booming capitalist endeavour.

The Hauptwerk site had been divided into two by a central spine road running east-west. Most of the significant buildings were north of this divide. To the south, it was concluded, large-scale clearance could take place and most of the buildings there were sold to a developer as the site for a hotel, retail centre and offices. Only the listed buildings were kept. To the north, more limited clearance was envisaged under a 1992 DEGW masterplan, itself the product of a series of workshop sessions with the client, potential investors, the university and the local community.

The development of the buildings had to be carried forward with another consultant appointed by the client, the Stuttgart-based IFB group. The latter was responsible for the demonstrative revamp of the former 1959 research building as prestige offices. The university has occupied other parts of the site, while the former works fire station was refurbished by DEGW as an investor centre with exhibits

A historic observatory, built by Carl Zeiss on top of one of the original buildings, has been refurbished. Its dome inspired the form of the new galleria below.

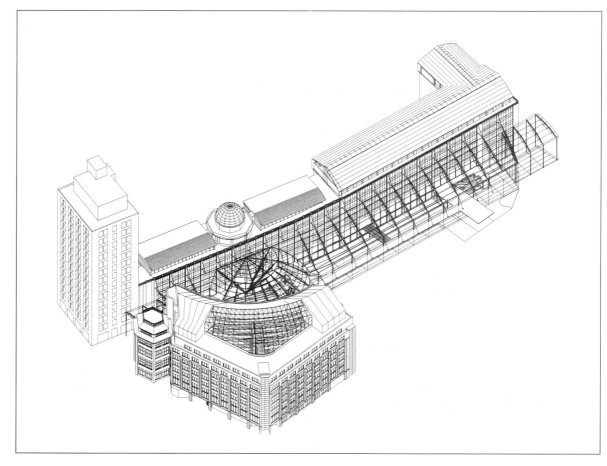

The Goethe Galerie, as it is now known, is firmly placed within a well-tried engineering tradition and forms a logical new element in this former industrial site.

for potential investors, tenants and the general public. DEGW was also responsible for the rehabilitation of the Hochhaus as offices for Jen-Optik and for an entirely new hotel.

But the centrepiece of the entire development is undoubtedly DEGW's Goethe Galerie, extending along the line of the original spine road that bisects the site. At street level this great glazed arcade, 140 metres long and culminating in a

domed central space, contains shops. Above are entrances to the office buildings and hotel. The Galerie reflects DEGW's ability to see a project through from initial research, through masterplan and briefing to completed buildings. The virtuoso use of glazing seems particularly appropriate in this location, given the great tradition of Carl Zeiss. DEGW had initially envisaged the spine road remaining open to the sky as a pedestri-

an route, but the large scale of the adjoining buildings made it a rather unappealing and dark space so the idea of an arcade emerged.

From brief, to masterplan, to buildings, Jena demonstrates not only DEGW's range but equally its holistic approach. The changing city might seem to threaten old and established ways but, equally, it marks the way to the future.

The glazing of
the Goethe Gal-
erie was design-
ed in association
with engineer-
architect IFB Dr
Braschel GmbH
and incorporates
the latest tech-
nology – appro-
priate to a site
where advances
in the use of
glass were pio-
neered.

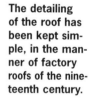

The detailing
of the roof has
been kept sim-
ple, in the man-
ner of factory
roofs of the nine-
teenth century.

Reaching out and
inviting passers-
by to enter, the
entrance canopy
of the hotel *(left)*
reflects the glaz-
ed roof of the
Goethe Galerie
(far left), the
central space of
which acts as a
clear symbol of
regeneration.

Futures

What is really special about DEGW? What is the particular contribution that the practice has made to contemporary architectural practice and to architectural ideas? Undoubtedly, there are many unusual features about DEGW, for example the bedrock of cumulative experience that a long history of specialisation in one building type has created; the co-existence of strong design and vigorous consultancy; a bias towards international and corporate clients combined with expertise in local, popular and participative design processes; the contribution to international debate through the regular publication of books, articles and research papers; and a network of offices that extends from London to Glasgow, from Paris to Milan, and from Sydney to New York. But are these features different enough to distinguish

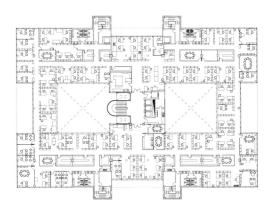

DEGW now has offices all over Europe. This is the new office for Cubiertas, for which DEGW España advised on all aspects of space planning, from brief to fit-out.

DEGW from dozens of other practices, particularly against the backdrop of the varied, inventive and sometimes sensationally successful architecture of the late twentieth century?

Individually, of course, none of these features is. It is, instead, the way they have been combined and woven together over almost three decades of deliberate development. What is truly radical in DEGW's work, and is of greatest benefit to its clients, is the systematic use of architectural practice as an intellectual as well as an artistic device to explore the probable shape of a changing world.

Exploring the future has always been one of the prime roles of architecture. Designing such long-term artifacts as buildings inevitably puts pressure on architects to look into the future. Magnificent examples of innovative, often utopian, architecture can be found in practically every era. However, architectural innovation does not have a consistently good name, particularly with clients, since innovation is often confused with searching for novel styles or striking unconventional attitudes. The cool, systematic and deliberate investigation of future options is not as common as it ought to be.

This means that, although most architects individually like to think of themselves as innovators, architectural practice, on the whole, tends to be conservative, following rather than initiating social change. There are cogent reasons for

this trend towards stasis. Among the powerful economic forces that tend to push architecture towards being frozen and timeless are construction processes that seek to minimise risk in the short term and, more often than not, inadvertently close down longer term options for clients.

Many architects feel strongly that they have to protect themselves – and indeed their clients – against change in the form of shifting and open-ended user politics or social and political fluidity in the planning process. Because architects are rewarded for 'getting it right on the night' they have not been particularly good at providing the kinds of environmental conditions that respond to changing user demands and to changing patterns of use. Architectural imagery, and particularly architectural photography, show all too clearly that conventional architectural practice finds it difficult to cope with the messy, the personal and the open-ended – in short, it finds it hard to cope with any form of change.

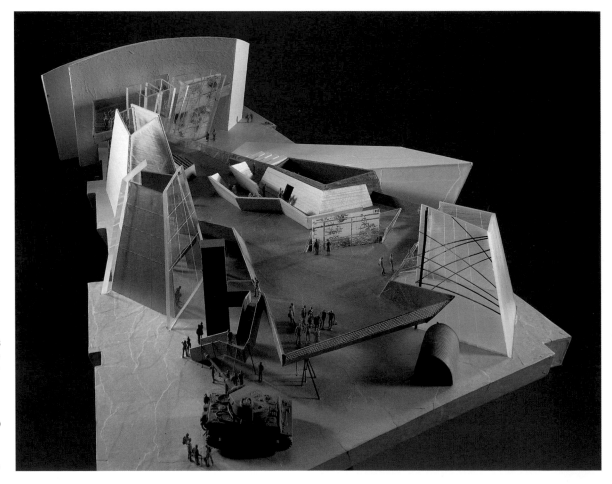

Daniel Libeskind's competition-winning proposal for the War Museum of the North, at Trafford. DEGW worked with Bob Baxter to prepare the exhibition masterplan.

What characterises all DEGW's work is an ongoing fascination with exactly the opposite: exploring the changes that society, clients and users are experiencing or anticipating, and then inventing architectural forms and delivery processes that respond to and accommodate change. This leads to a rational iconoclasm that rejects many of the physical forms of conventional architecture as well as many of the processes by which it is shaped – and distorted. Such productive scepticism encourages innovation in strategic planning,

design and procurement methods, all of which lead to better ways of measuring the success of buildings and cities, and of predicting their future performance.

The consequence is that DEGW is prolific in areas that many architects consider – quite wrongly – to be peripheral to real architecture. For example, DEGW is developing fresh urban design procedures because without long-term strategies short-term change cannot be accommodated. DEGW is pioneering new briefing and programming techniques to make the control of

166

Below: the main banking hall of the old National Westminster Bank building in London, refurbished by DEGW to form the Lothbury Gallery.

building design accessible to ever-changing user demand. DEGW continues to champion facilities management because, to make change in buildings possible, procedures and protocols must be created to anticipate and respond to emerging user demands. DEGW also advocates post-occupancy evaluation because, without relating actual building performance to initial and emerging client objectives, architecture is blind. Finally, DEGW continues to invent numerous ways of measuring building performance, to record discrepancies between what is and what ought to be. Without such comparisons, directing and managing change in building use is meaningless and, of course, practically impossible.

DEGW is impatient with the supply-side thinking that characterises conventional construction and real estate, which so often subordinates user priorities to easy delivery and quick deals. The case studies in this book demonstrate the extent to which DEGW has contributed to improving the ways that buildings are procured and built: the Ministry of Defence, Andersen Consulting and Andersen Worldwide in briefing; the Department of Trade and Industry in construction; and Boots the Chemists and Great Ormond Street Hospital in designing new ways of facilitating change.

DEGW's collaborative work with many other architects is continually strengthening the practice's experience, not only in design itself but also in design management and building procurement.

Similarly, three decades of exposure to the rigours and disciplines of interior design for corporate offices – in which responsiveness to changing and demanding users is so critical – have proved an important influence on DEGW's continuing desire to design for change. In recent years, this rich seam of experience, and the diagnostic techniques and methods which it has generated, has been translated with increasing frequency into other related sectors – libraries, teaching establishments, laboratories, museums and so on – as information technology has increased the convergence between learning and working environments. This series of innovations has been achieved by understanding that the practice is a kind of 'knowledge engine', which works best when it transcends the achievements of individual projects.

DEGW is sometimes compared to a university with an ongoing intellectual and research programme. This is an attractive metaphor but not a totally accurate one because it is only in practice, only in the highly turbulent context of action with real clients and real data and real changes, that DEGW finds it possible to accumulate the particular expertise, the special knowledge, the searching questions that are so necessary to satisfy our priorities and to develop our particular, open-ended line of enquiry into how designing for change should affect architectural procedures and ultimately architectural form.

What makes DEGW special is an intellectual and artistic climate in which research and design, consultancy and practice, are deliberately

DEGW's recently refurbished London office at Porters North. Standing-height tables facilitate short meetings over drawings in the new project team areas.

juxtaposed to challenge and complement one another. Everything that is researched must be driven through to its ultimate conclusion in physical design; everything that is designed must stem from and test some research finding or consultancy recommendation. This is the momentum that drives us to explore how architectural practice can support speculation in the context of action. It is for this reason that DEGW is evolving, with Twijnstra Gudde, from an architectural partnership into a collective of knowledge-based professionals.

This climate continues to stimulate a body of work that is distinctive in two ways: first, as an important but not always immediately visible

To promote greater mobility, DEGW has introduced cordless telephones and PCs that can be plugged into the central network anywhere.

contribution – at least in conventional architectural terms – about understanding changing user needs to learn how to programme, design and manage working environments that can accommodate such changes; and second, with a sequence of highly visible urban, architectural and interior

design projects that test, illustrate and demonstrate how change can be accommodated in elegant and practical ways.

The idea of linking the understanding of changing user needs with the invention of an appropriate architecture is what has always characterised DEGW projects. It can be seen in much of the practice's current work: a training centre for Shell, in the Netherlands, that seeks to serve two entirely different uses within the same space; a multi-client study in Latin America that is exploring the urban consequences of networked information technology; a jewel of an office building for the Japanese company Taisei, in a corner of Mayfair, that packs into a tiny compass everything that we have learned about accommodating changing tenant needs; a brief, not just for the accommodation, but for restructuring the Organisation for Economic Cooperation and Development, one of the most important major international organisations in Paris; a strategic masterplan for the redesign of Utrecht that responds to the emerging potential of new transportation systems; and our own new offices in London that demonstrate the aesthetic as well as the practical potential of new ways of working.

However, the one really distinctive contribution of DEGW, the principal feature of the practice that makes it a model for knowledge-based architectural practices of the future, is that these two strands of work – consultancy and design – are intentionally and completely intertwined, complementary and dependent upon each other. It is the symbiotic combination of these two strands that has made possible the systematic modelling and testing of the architectural consequences of change. DEGW is reinventing architectural practice to make it a powerful form of intellectual and artistic enquiry in its own right. In a time of accelerating change, this can be achieved in no other way.

Redefining the club. The centre of DEGW's new office is designed to accommodate visitors and 'nomads' – the more itinerant staff members who need somewhere to sit, to talk, to think, to read and to sort themselves out between meetings.

Porters North has become a richer, more lively environment because it now provides a wide variety of settings which can accommodate many complex tasks: some highly interactive, others requiring a good deal of concentration and privacy.

171

Key Projects

1971-1975

Offices & Principals

JFN 1971-74
DLGW 1974-76
Wigmore Street
London

Brussels (JFN)
New York (JFN)

Colin Cave
Francis Duffy
Peter Eley
Luigi Giffone
Alex Lange
John Worthington

(Alex Lange leaves in 1974)

Design Projects

Sharp MacManus,
London: *office interiors*

Smith Barney, London:
interiors

Burton Group:
prototype shops

English & Continental,
London: *interiors*

American Express,
Cannon Street, London:
interiors

Christies, King Street
and South Kensington,
London: *salesrooms*

IBM, Amsterdam: *PAC
office interiors*

IBM Segrate, Milan:
interior consultancy

Architecture &
Planning

Rotherhithe, London:
*reuse of redundant
buildings*

Covent Garden, London:
regeneration studies
(with URBED)

Research &
Consultancy

Government Offices:
space standards review
(for MPBW)

CEGB, Stockport: *brief
and layouts*

IBM Segrate, Milan:
space planning

South West Water
Authority, Exeter:
office planning

Concepts &
Publications

Space planning

*Shell, Structure,
Services, Scenery,
Settings*

Space Budgeting

Local area stocktaking

*'AA' Office Planning
conference, 1971*

**Planning Office
Space** series for *The
Architects' Journal*

**Princeton Disserta-
tion**, Francis Duffy,
1974

1976-1980

Offices & Principals	Design Projects	Architecture & Planning	Research & Consultancy	Concepts & Publications
DEGW Welbeck St, London W1	Digital European HQ, Geneva: *interiors*	Basildon: *housing and retail*	American Express, Haywards Heath : *space planning*	*Facilities management*
Building Use Studies (*with* ABK)	Unipart Factory, Coventry: *interiors*	BNFL, Warrington: new headquarters	IBM UK branch offices: *space planning*	*Fin walls – combined servicing and space planning*
Colin Cave Francis Duffy Peter Eley Luigi Giffone John Worthington	Factory Mutual, London: *office interiors* Christies, New York, Amsterdam and Glasgow: *salerooms*		IBM Netherlands: *sales office studies* BNFL, Warrington: *lighting studies* Welsh Development Agency: *brief for science parks* Genesis Project, Warrington: *brief* NKR, Sweden: *'Office of the Future' furniture brief* IBM Europe: *open-plan study* Wiggins Teape, Basingstoke: *space planning* Hackney and Islington, London: *redundant buildings studies* (*with* URBED)	*Premises ladder* *Redundant building appraisal methodology* *Three-zone office buildings – intermediate air technology* *Tenant profiles and handbooks* *'Management Centre of Europe' conferences in Brussels, Amsterdam, Munich, Paris etc.* (*with* Congena) **Planning Office Space**, Duffy, Cave, Worthington, 1976 **Industrial Rehabilitation**, Eley & Worthington, 1979

1981-1985

Offices & Principals

DEGW Partnership
Bulstrode Place
London W1

Mexico City 1981-87
Paris 1981 (joint venture
with Espace Architecture)
Glasgow 1983
Milan 1984

Building Use Studies

Colin Cave
Francis Duffy
Peter Eley
Luigi Giffone
John Worthington

Design Projects

ESB Headquarters,
Dublin: *interiors*

Thenamaris, Athens:
interiors

IBM, Basingstoke:
interiors

IBM Hursley, Block DX:
interiors

Ernst & Young, London:
interiors

Sturge, London:
interiors

CAP, London: *interiors*

Wang, London:
interiors

Locate in Scotland,
Glasgow: *interiors*

Barclays Bank, Fleet-
way House, London:
interiors

La Rinascente, Milan:
office interiors

Digital, Valbonne:
interiors

Wiggins Teape 2,
Basingstoke: *brief,
space planning and
interiors*

Architecture & Planning

BNFL, Warrington: *HQ
completed*

Stockley Park, Middle-
sex: *masterplan com-
petition winner*

House for Colin Cave,
London

Welsh Development
Agency, Newport: *multi-
occupancy scheme
design*

Research & Consultancy

ORBIT 1 UK
(first multi-client study)

ORBIT 2 North America

Hewlett Packard UK:
*desk sharing studies
and prototype layouts*
(with Herman Miller)

South Shoreditch, Lon-
don: *planning studies*

Dundee Technology
Park: *brief*

IBM UK: *brief for
branch offices*

Barclays Bank, UK:
branch studies

Cutlers Gardens, Lon-
don: *tenant profiles*

IBM Hursley: *master-
planning*

IBM Semea, Milan:
*space planning and
strategic consultancy*

Concepts & Publications

Multi-client studies

Building Appraisals
(first applied at Finsbury Avenue)

*Property strategies for
health service buildings*
(by John Worthington)

*Sick building syndrome
studies*

Courses in space plan-
ning at the University
of Cincinnati

**Eleven Contemporary
Office Buildings**, for
Rosehaugh Stanhope,
1985

**Premises of Excel-
lence**, Wilson & Strelitz,
1986 (BUS and DEGW)

Facilities Newsletter,
founded 1984

**Meeting the Needs
of Modern Industry**,
for Stockley Park, 1985

Trading in Two Cities,
for Rosehaugh Stan-
hope, 1985

**Architectural Com-
petition Guidelines**,
DoE and RIBA, 1985

1986-1990

Offices & Principals	Design Projects	Architecture & Planning	Research & Consultancy	Concepts & Publications
DEGW Crinan Street London N1 Glasgow Milan Madrid Paris Building Use Studies DEGW T3 DEGW Net Hugh Anderson Chris Byng-Maddick Colin Cave Francis Duffy Peter Eley John Francis Luigi Giffone David Jenkin Luigi V Mangano John Worthington (Luigi Giffone retires) (Partnership ends and DEGW incorporated in 1989)	Lloyds Bank, Hays Galleria, London: *interiors* (Office of the Year Award) Lloyd's of London, 1958 Building: *interiors* Freshfields, London: *interiors* First National Bank, London: *interiors* First Interstate Bank, London: *interiors* Agip, Jacorossi, Rome: *interiors* Philips, Madrid: *interiors* SVP HQ, St Ouen, France: *interiors* Digital France, Evry: *interiors*	Pudding Lane, London: *office building* Appold Street, London: *office reconstruction* Rosehaugh, London: *Marylebone Lane office building* Wootton Basset, Wiltshire: *industrial buildings* Trafalgar House, London: *speculative office building* Le Mans, France: *business park masterplan* Kajima, Tokyo: *urban design studies* Denkfabrik, Berlin: *competition-winning project* Roissy Pole, Paris: *development brief* CNTS, Les Ulis, France: *headquarters building* Merchant City, Glasgow: *planning studies* San Fernando, Madrid: *business park masterplan* Babelsburg Film Studio, Berlin: *strategic brief*	Broadgate, London: *user research* Stockley Park, Middlesex: *user research and planning studies* Lloyds Bank UK: *branch studies* London Underground: *design guidelines* Royal Docks, London: *design guidelines* Prudential HQ, London: *brief* Le Monde HQ, Paris: *space planning* IBM UK: *NOSS and SMART studies* Department of Education & Science: *educational building studies* EBRD, London: *site selection studies* Trafalgar House business parks, UK: *briefs* ITN, London: *brief* Broadgate and Wates City Tower, London: *post-occupancy evaluation* Chiswick Park, London: *user studies and brief* King's Cross Redevelopment, London: *briefing studies* Paternoster Square, London: *competition brief* IBM Milan: *space planning and strategic consultancy* J Walter Thompson, Milan: *building evaluation and space planning* Procter and Gamble, Rome: *building evaluation and space planning* Medi-Park, Erskine: *brief*	*Sectoral studies* *International comparative studies of client requirements* *Action Planning* *Intelligent Building studies* *Post-occupancy evaluation* DEGW Berlin: *first presentations* The City of Birmingham: *Highbury Initiatives* Stockley Park and Broadgate, London: *tenant guides* Lloyds Bank, Hays Lane House: *user guides* **The Changing City**, Duffy and Henney, 1989 **Developing Business Success**, Trafalgar House, 1988 **Trading in Three Cities**, Rosehaugh Stanhope, 1991 **Intelligent Building in Europe – executive summary**, British Council of Offices, 1992

Publications

1974   *Office Interiors and Organisations*, Princeton University

1976   *Planning Office Space*, Architectural Press

1979   *Oficinas*, Blume

1982   *The Office Book*, Facts on File

1983   *ORBIT 1,* DEGW/BUS/Eosys *Facilities*, Bulstrode Press

1984   *Industrial Rehabilitation*, Architectural Press
L'Empire du Bureau, CNAP Berger Levrault

1985   *ORBIT 2*, DEGW/Harbinger/Facilities Research Associates
Eleven Contemporary Office Buildings, Rosehaugh Stanhope
Meeting the Needs of Modern Industry, Stockley plc

1986   *A Working Guide to Stockley Park*, Stockley plc
Trading in Two Cities, Rosehaugh Stanhope
Architectural Competitions: RIBA Code of Practice, RIBA

1987   *Developing Business Success*, Trafalgar House Developments
Architectural Competitions Briefing, Bulstrode Press
Paternoster Square Urban Design Competition: Briefing Document, DEGW

1988   *Fitting Out the Workplace*, Architectural Press
Trading in Three Cities, Rosehaugh Stanhope
Broadgate: a working guide, Rosehaugh Stanhope

1989   *The Changing City*, Bulstrode Press
Information Technology and Buildings, Butler Cox
Créer les Espaces de Bureaux, Strafor/Nathan
Operating Your Business at Stockley Park, Heathrow, Stockley plc
IBM Space Occupancy Study, IBM UK
London Underground Station Environment Guidelines, London Underground

1990   *The Human Office*, CSK Japan
The Responsive Office, Steelcase Strafor / Polymath
Design Guidelines for Professional Offices, Rosehaugh Stanhope

1991   *Interior Design of the Electronic Office*, Van Nostrand Reinhold
Guide de l'Aménagement de Bureaux, Le Moniteur

1992   *The Intelligent Building in Europe*, multi-client study with Teknibank
The Changing Workplace, Phaidon

1993   *The Responsible Workplace*, Butterworth Heinemann

1994   *South Bank Centre Urban Design Competition Brief*, DEGW

1995   *New Environments for Working*, multi-client study with The Building Research Establishment

1996   *Intelligent Buildings in South East Asia*, multi-client study with Ove Arup & Partners and Northcroft

Heritage and Technology, New ways of working in historic buildings, DEGW / Lucent Technologies / English Heritage
Intelligence At Work, Olivetti

1997   *Reinventing the Workplace*, Architectural Press
The New Office, Conran Octopus

1998   *Intelligent Buildings in Latin America*, multi-client study with Ove Arup & Partners and Northcroft
Intelligent Buildings in South East Asia, E&FN Spon
Architectural Knowledge: The Idea of a Profession, E&FN Spon
New Environments for Working, E&FN Spon

Credits